Your
Dog
Interpreter

Your Dog Interpreter

How to Understand Man's Best Friend

David Alderton

Reader's Digest

The Reader's Digest Association, Inc.
Pleasantville, New York / Montreal

A READER'S DIGEST BOOK

This edition published by The Reader's Digest Association, Inc., by arrangement with Cico Books, an imprint of Ryland Peters and Small Ltd
20—21 Jockey's Fields, London WC1R 4BW

Copyright © 2007 Cico Books

FOR CICO BOOKS
Design Jerry Goldie
Editor Marie Clayton
Illustrators Cathy Brear, Trina Dalziel
Photo Credits see page 192

FOR READER'S DIGEST
U.S. Project Editor Barbara Booth
Canadian Project Editor Pamela Johnson
Project Designer Jennifer Tokarski
Associate Art Director George McKeon
Executive Editor, Trade Publishing Dolores York
Associate Publisher Rosanne McManus
President and Publisher, Trade Publishing
    Harold Clarke

Alderton, David, 1956–
    Your dog interpreter : how to understand man's best friend
/ David Alderton.
        p. cm.
    ISBN 0-7621-855-X (978-0-7621-0885-8)
  1. Dogs--Behavior. 2. Dogs. 3. Human-animal communication.
I. Title.
  SF433.A45 2007
  636.7--dc22   2007022098

Address any comments about *Your Dog Interpreter* to:
        The Reader's Digest Association, Inc.
        Adult Trade Publishing
        Reader's Digest Road
        Pleasantville, NY 10570-7000

For more Reader's Digest products and information, visit our website:
        www.rd.com (in the United States)
        www.readersdigest.ca (in Canada)

NOTES TO OUR READERS
The advice given here should not be used as a substitute for that of a qualified veterinarian. No dogs or puppies were harmed in the making of this book.

In this book, unless the information given is specifically for female dogs, dogs are referred to as "he." The information is equally applicable to male and female dogs, unless otherwise specified.

Printed in China

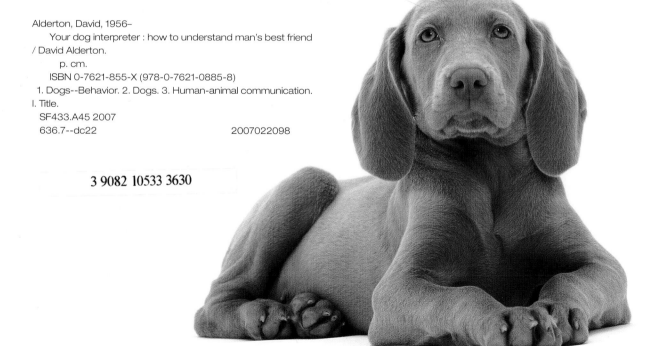

Contents

Canine
Companionship

The bond between people and dogs stretches back beyond the start

of recorded history—for at least 15,000 years and possibly nearer to

100,000 years. At the start, their relationship was utilitarian, with

dogs helping to hunt, warning of danger, and even being eaten if food

was otherwise in short supply. However, archaeology has revealed

clear signs that dogs soon became cherished companions as well as

working animals, and since those early days, people and dogs have

continued to maintain a close relationship.

From Working Animal to Pet

Certain breeds were evolved for specific work purposes. However, the view of dogs as a household companion selected for its looks came about in the late 1800s as a result of the dog show.

The most dramatic shift in man's relationship with canines has occurred over the past century, because the majority of dogs are now no longer kept as working companions but simply as pets. This has caused difficulties, because breeds that had been developed over the course of many centuries as workers cannot easily abandon their ancestral past to settle only as household companions. Collies, for example, have worked as sheepdogs for many thousands of years and can very easily become bored and even destructive without having sufficient exercise and distraction. This is why it is vital that you delve carefully into the ancestry of breeds that interest you to gain a clear insight into their behavior before taking on a canine companion, rather than simply being seduced by a cute appearance. You need to match the needs of your pet to your lifestyle to ensure that—as much as possible—you will be compatible with each other.

All dogs are individuals, just as we are, and experiences gained through life shape their personalities. If you are not used to having dogs around, it may be better to start with a puppy who can grow up in your home, rather

than taking on an adult dog from an animal shelter who will already have set behavior patterns. There are a number of people—such as your veterinarian or a local dog trainer—who will be able to guide you through the critical early months if you have not had a puppy before, helping to ensure that your pet will grow up to be a well-trained companion. Some breeds, such as the whippet, are much more responsive to training than others, such as the chow chow, and this is another important factor to consider at the outset when determining which type of dog to choose.

Some General Canine Characteristics

Within their various groups, dogs have certain traits in common.

Gundogs: Responsive but active. Can be prone to obesity without adequate exercise.

Scent hounds: Enthusiastic and exuberant. Running off can be a problem.

Sheepdogs: Intelligent, active companions that respond well to training.

Sight hounds: Often sleek-coated, so grooming needs are minimal. Like to run. Can be nervous with strangers.

Terriers: Lively, feisty dogs with plenty of energy. Often dig and can bark loudly.

The Influence of Dog Shows

The way that we view dogs has also altered significantly since the 1800s, to some extent mirroring changes in society, and is continuing to do so today. The industrialization that swept through Europe and North America during the second half of the 1800s gave rise to a growing and increasingly prosperous middle class. This in turn led to the phenomenon known as "fancying"—the selective breeding of plants and animals, with competitions in which entrants were judged against an ideal to select a winner. It was quite natural that dogs would form part of this trend, since they had been closely involved with people over the course of many centuries.

An Englishman, Charles Cruft, initially appreciated the scope of the dog fancy when he visited a show being staged as part of the Paris Exhibition in 1878. He returned home full of inspiration, organized a terrier show with the backing of wealthy dog-loving patrons, and by 1891 was sufficiently confident to launch an annual show for all breeds. The public was soon flocking to these events, keen to see the ever growing number of different types of dog on display. The dog was no longer perceived as a working companion but as an object of aesthetic pleasure, and not surprisingly, more people started to acquire them. One contemporary estimate suggested that dog ownership had risen more than sixty-fold between the late 1800s and the early 1900s. This was almost certainly an exaggeration, but this period undoubtedly saw the establishment of the dog as a household companion and reflected a trend that has continued right through to the present day. Alongside this growth in ownership, the supply of prepared dog food—which was pioneered by James Spratt and Charles Cruft himself—has also grown into a massive global industry.

Changing Perspectives

Artists of the time captured the growing sentimental feeling toward dogs, a trend that began in late Victorian times. It helped, of course, that members of the British royal family—including Queen Victoria herself—were known to be great dog lovers. The loyalty of a dog toward his owner was reflected by many contemporary portrayals of the period by artists such as Sir Edwin Landseer. Later artists, such as Arthur Wardle, tended to emphasize the beauty and form of the dog after show standards became well established. Shows themselves were social occasions, drawing people from a variety of backgrounds. The progression of the dog to the show ring and, later, to fireside companion followed a similar pattern in North America, with the establishment of the American Kennel Club in 1884 and its Canadian counterpart four years later.

Hollywood Dogs

In America a new medium—that of cinematic film—was growing in authority and would bring the appeal of owning a dog to an ever wider audience. In its early days, Hollywood made stars out of several dogs— starting with Rin Tin Tin in the 1920s.

Rin Tin Tin

When an American airman, Lee Duncan, rescued a German shepherd puppy from an abandoned dugout in France at the end of the First World War, little did he realize how this display of kindness would transform his life. Back in California, Rinty easily mastered a number of tricks that his owner taught him, so when Duncan heard that a film company was looking for a dog to play a part in one of their movies, he decided to take Rinty along for the audition. He

Fashion does influence the popularity of breeds, causing them to undergo shifts in their popularity. Fox terriers, like this wire-coated example, were very popular in the 1920s, but their numbers have since declined significantly over the years.

didn't expect to be successful—he just wanted to go and see how a film studio operated.

However, Rinty—named after a small doll that French soldiers had carried for luck during the war—won the part. The resulting movie, *Where the North Begins*, was released in 1923 and was an immense hit, mainly because of Rinty's contribution. It was the start of a career that saw Rin Tin Tin earning over 5 million dollars—a huge amount of money even today—and at the peak of his fame receiving 10,000 letters from fans every week. Some in the film industry even regarded Rin Tin Tin as the savior of the famous Warner Brothers studios. Although rival studios tried to copy

the format, they were mostly unsuccessful—as far as the public was concerned, there was only one Rin Tin Tin. He made 19 feature films, as well as starring in a number of mini series, and when he died in 1932, his son maintained the family tradition—although he remained firmly in the shadow of his famous father.

Lassie

While Rin Tin Tin remains the most famous individual dog ever to star in a movie, there have been other famous film parts for dogs, which have reinforced their popular standing as faithful companions. The best known are the *Lassie* films, the origins of which can be traced back to a short

Dogs soon learn to adapt to family living, especially if acquired as puppies.

story entitled "Lassie Come Home," which was originally published in a British newspaper in 1938 but was expanded into a book some two years later. It told the story of a boy, Joe, who was accompanied back from school every day for four years by his faithful pet dog, Lassie. However, the two were separated when Joe's father was forced to sell the dog because they could no longer afford to feed her. Lassie went away to a new home that was more than 400 miles away, but courageously she headed back in search of her old home, finally being reunited with Joe after a series of dramatic events.

A film based on the book was released in 1943, starring a rough collie called Pal, who was propelled into the role at the last minute after the producers' first choice molted

Two breeds whose popularity has been boosted as a result of starring film roles are the German shepherd (below), which used to be known as the Alsatian, and the rough collie (opposite).

most of her long coat just prior to the start of filming in the summer. The movie proved very popular, diverting people from the grim realities of the Second World War, which was then raging across Europe and beyond. Pal himself continued in the role for a further six films and also took part in a radio show that featured Lassie barking dutifully at appropriate moments. Four generations of Pal's descendants subsequently assumed the role in various revivals between 1953 and 1974. The last dog actually related to Pal appeared in the part in 1978, but the enduring fascination of Lassie is such that new versions of the story continue to be filmed, both for the cinema and for television.

By the 1950s, however, life had become rather more complicated, as reflected by Fred Gipson's story of Old Yeller, which was subsequently turned into a film by Walt Disney. Here was a tough, ugly cross breed, living up to his name in both color and voice and missing an ear, who comes into the life of a Texas frontier family in the 1860s by stealing some meat. Old Yeller continues to hang around, and a growing bond between him and the family is significantly strengthened when he saves the older boy, Travis, from being badly savaged by a group of wild boar, suffering dreadful injuries himself in the process.

At the end of the story, he battles with a rabid wolf, defending Travis's mother from certain death, but then must be shot by the family to prevent

him from suffering the symptoms of this dreadful, incurable disease. Here was not only unswerving loyalty but also redemption.

Even in the more overtly cynical mood that seems to prevail today, filmmakers have not neglected the role of the dog as a force for good in our lives. This was even apparent in the movie *Cats and Dogs*, released early in 2001, which placed the traditional images of these two popular groups of pets into sharp contrast: It features loyal dogs seeking to protect human endeavor from opportunistic cats.

Mirrors of Society

Various writers have also explored the possibility of gaining a wider insight into the world around us—good or bad—through sharing one's life with a dog. John Steinbeck's *Travels with Charley: In Search of America* was published in 1962 and revealed deep-seated social divisions in North American society in that period.

Subsequently, *Travels with Lizbeth: Three Years on the Road and on the Streets* by Lars Eighner appeared in 1993. He describes how he grew to rely on Lizbeth's abilities while they were living rough together: Both had effectively been cast out by society, but together they formed a team with a strong and meaningful bond growing between them.

"Brand" Celebrities

In the past, dogs became famous through the media for their starring role in a film or because they had well-known owners, but now there is a new dimension becoming evident. At the start of the 21st century, the phenomenon of dogs evolving into brand celebrities in their own right marks another turning point in our relationship with our canine companions. The links between fashion and personalities that have developed in human society are now being reflected in canine circles as

Nipper

Of course, in the past, specific dogs have become linked with particular brands and used to sell the brand to the public. The most notable example was probably Nipper, a black-and-white fox terrier. Nipper was born in 1884 and came into the care of the artist Francis Barraud after his original owner died. Barraud was entranced by the way that Nipper would sit and cock his ear in the direction of the gramophone when music was playing and the artist painted the scene, entitling the work "His Master's Voice."

Initially, Barraud was unable to sell the painting, but subsequently he updated it and in 1901 the Victor Talking Machine Company of Camden, New Jersey, acquired the American rights to both the picture and its title. This passed in due course to RCA when the companies merged, and Barraud's image of Nipper ultimately became the most famous and enduring symbol of recorded music throughout the 20th century. Nipper died in 1895, however, before he could enjoy his newfound fame.

well, with anthropomorphism growing in strength.

International fashion brands for dogs are being created and are promoted by particular dogs, portrayed as canine celebrities. Manfred, a Yorkshire terrier from the Swedish town of Malmo, is a leading figure in this movement. The media spotlight is very much on Manfred and his clothing range, which is being presented as high-end canine fashion. He has visited Hollywood, met with film stars, and is treated as a canine celebrity whenever he attends events. The result is that Manfred has helped to create both an exclusive and an aspirational brand, directly reflecting the way in which certain designer labels for people are marketed.

Manfred of Sweden, wearing a nautical outfit, is one of the modern stars of the contemporary dog world, and has become a leading fashion icon.

The appeal of dogs—especially puppies—is such that they are frequently used to advertise a wide range of products.

Dogs and Their Personalities

It is only very recently that dogs have crossed the threshold to live as our companions indoors. They were originally regarded mainly as working animals, and the jobs for which they were bred have shaped their personalities. This is why it is important to look at the ancestry of breeds that appeal to you rather than to select a dog simply on the basis of looks, because you may find out that its temperament does not suit your surroundings and lifestyle.

What Are Breeds?

Nobody can say definitely how many breeds of dog there are, because of the definition of what constitutes a breed. Essentially, a recognizable breed is a type of dog with distinctive physical characteristics whose puppies will have the same traits. All the major characteristics of the breed are summarized in their show standard, which judges use at dog shows to determine the winners of specific classes. On this basis, only types of dog that have recognized judging standards can be counted as breeds, and there are around 250 breeds that are recognized worldwide for show purposes.

A broader definition of a breed is a recognizable type of dog that produces puppies that clearly resemble it, and there are as many as another 150 distinctive types of dog covered by this broader definition. These other breeds usually have a very localized distribution and are still kept

Dognosis
Different Breeds

There is no universal classification of dog breeds. However, show classifications tend to divide dogs into distinct groups that reflect the purpose for which they have been bred and thus their characteristic behavior. Hounds, for example, may be further divided into sight hounds and scent hounds. There are also usually the terriers, a toy group, a herding or pastoral group, and a sporting or gundog division. When considering a particular breed, the show categories can provide insight into a dog's likely behavior, and whether it is suited to urban living or should be kept only in a rural area.

for working purposes but are not likely to be seen in the show ring. In time, however, their popularity may spread, so they in turn establish a more widespread following. At this point they will start to be seen in the show ring, and a show standard will therefore be established.

Dogs come in all shapes and sizes, but all are descended from the gray wolf. Those that are standard in appearance represent breeds. All others are often simply described as mutts—such as the one at the end of the line of hounds and terriers below!

Hounds

Hounds represent probably the oldest of all dog lineages, having been around for about a thousand years. Within this category the two biggest groups are the sight hounds and the scent hounds, and they can usually be distinguished by their appearance.

Sight Hounds

Sight hounds have relatively long, narrow noses and an athletic build. They tend to be short-coated, although there are exceptions, such as the saluki. The coloration of sight hounds tends to be more variable than that of scent hounds, and a number have single-color coats. They form a strong bond with their owners and generally require less exercise than scent hounds. They are able to sprint at a blistering pace—whippets, sometimes described as a poor man's racehorse, are able to accelerate to 35 mph (56 kph) over short distances.

Sight hounds have very acute vision and can spot movement from a considerable distance away, so they may disappear very rapidly into the distance if, for instance, a rabbit emerges on the horizon. You will need to keep a close watch because once they launch into pursuit of their quarry, everything is over very quickly—before you can do anything, in fact. Sight hounds are usually shyer than scent hounds, so they are likely to be slightly nervous by nature, especially when encountering strangers.

Greyhound

Many ex-racing greyhounds need homes after their career on the track; they are very gentle dogs and make excellent companions. However, they do display a strong hunting instinct—they need to be muzzled in public places because they may chase and catch small dogs, mistaking them for rabbits. Contrary to popular belief, greyhounds need very little exercise—a brisk run once or twice a day is adequate.

Afghan Hound

Most sight hounds are short-coated and have minimal grooming needs, although the Afghan hound has a coat that has grown longer due to selective

The Afghan hound is a very graceful breed, with a more profuse coat today than in the past. Usually displaying remarkable agility, the Afghan hound also has plenty of stamina.

Easy-to-Train Breeds

- Australian shepherd
- Border collie
- German shepherd
- Labrador retriever
- Rough collie
- Shetland sheepdog
- Smooth collie

Harder-to-Train Breeds

- Afghan hound
- Basset hound
- Beagle
- Cardigan Welsh corgi
- Chow chow
- Irish setter

breeding in the West over the past 100 years or so. There were several strains, with those from desert areas being lighter in build and coat color than dogs from more mountainous regions of the country.

Lurcher

To make hounds more trainable and responsive when hunting, they were crossbred with collies and other dogs to create lurchers. Although lurchers are not recognized for showing by national kennel clubs because they vary so much in their appearance, depending on their ancestry, they still attract a dedicated following. Lurchers can be broadly divided into two groups: larger lurchers, bred from greyhound or deerhound stock, and

their smaller counterparts, which are the result of whippet crosses.

Lurchers were traditionally regarded as poachers' dogs, often dark in color, enabling them to blend into the background at night. They also work silently, another essential attribute to escape detection. The name "lurcher" originates from the old Romany language—"lur" meaning "thief." Lurchers make good companions, provided their need for exercise can be met, and they are generally more responsive to training than true, or purebred, hounds.

Scent Hounds

Scent hounds are muscular dogs, well suited to run at a fast pace and with considerable stamina, although they lack the explosive sprinting abilities of sight hounds. They have much broader noses, enabling them to pursue a scent that is days old.

Many scent-hound breeds originated in France. They are usually either bi- or tricolored, and their individual patterning is varied enough that huntsmen are able to recognize each dog in a pack. Scent hounds are social dogs by nature, which helps them to integrate well into family surroundings. They tend to be natural extroverts, getting along well with people in spite of their loud bark. They are enthusiastic, energetic, and

Lurchers vary a great deal in appearance but are intelligent, good-natured dogs that make excellent family pets.

Hounds and Their Origins

The earliest hounds can be traced to the Middle East, and the saluki appears on Egyptian tombs from as far back as 2100 B.C. Due to their strong sense of smell, hounds also gained popularity in Europe as hunting companions. New breeds developed in the United States after hounds were brought to the recently discovered country during European voyages of colonization.

Name	Origin	Personality	Type of hound
Greyhound	U.K.	Very affectionate	Sight hound
Basenji	Congo	Intelligent and independent	Sight hound
Basset hound	France	Calm and loyal	Scent hound
Black-and-Tan coonhound	U.S.	Brave and alert	Scent hound
Bloodhound	France	Relaxed and friendly	Scent hound
Saluki	Middle East	Intelligent	Sight hound
Borzoi	Russia	Quiet and gracious	Sight hound
Dachshund	Germany	Playful but stubborn	Scent hound
Afghan hound	Afghanistan	Stubborn and independent	Sight hound
Beagle	U.K.	Curious, good with children	Scent hound

quite tolerant, which means they are ideal for a home with children approaching their teenage years, who have plenty of energy. Relatively long periods of daily exercise are essential for most hounds but especially for scent hounds, because they are instinctively lively dogs.

Unfortunately, their instinct to follow a scent is overwhelming, which means that training is difficult. They tend to run off quite readily, especially in the countryside. It is not wise to chase after a scent hound if he sets off on a scent trail, because in many cases he will outrun you. Worse still, he will probably misinterpret your efforts to stop him from running, thinking instead that you are joining in with the chase, causing him to run even faster.

Bloodhounds were much more commonly seen at early dog shows, simply because they are not as fashionable today. They make very affectionate if sometimes stubborn companions, and their grooming requirements are minimal.

The highly unusual body shape of the dachshund led to the smooth-coated form being described as the "sausage dog." There are also long-coated and wire-haired variants, which exist in standard and miniature forms.

The best thing is to stop and call your dog back to you—or even head off in the opposite direction. With a hound puppy, it is important from the outset to train your pet to return when called in order to prevent later problems.

Living in packs means that scent hounds are tolerant of other dogs, but they are also rather greedy when feeding and will steal food that is left within reach. As well as raiding shopping bags on the floor, they will jump up onto chairs to take food left on a table. Their gluttony means they are susceptible to obesity, so it is vital to develop a suitable balance between food and exercise.

Bloodhound

The bloodhound is probably the oldest of the scent hounds, being descended from the ancient St. Hubert Hound, with an ancestry that can be traced back nearly 2,000 years. Its broad nostrils help to ensure this breed has unparalleled tracking skills, and these dogs are often used today by law-enforcement agencies for this purpose. Bloodhounds have a gentle nature but also require plenty of exercise.

Dachshund

Some dogs, due to their body type, have very specialized hunting skills. The short-legged, long-bodied appearance of the dachshund is not that of a typical hound; as such, these dogs were originally bred to hunt underground, and their physique enabled them to pursue badgers.

Water Dogs

Waterfowl were once an important source of food for those living in wetland areas. In an era before guns, birds were shot down with arrows, but reclaiming them could be difficult, so a range of dogs was created for this purpose. They are often distinguished by their coats, which are usually water-resistant, so the dog did not become soaked to the skin and chilled while working. A number of such breeds was created in different parts of Europe over the course of centuries. They had to be intelligent so they could be trained, but also able to swim well in what could be icy and treacherous waters.

The origins of water-dog breeds are believed to lie in France—the ancient breed known as the barbet was central to their development. The barbet had a reputation for retrieving shot waterfowl and bringing back the arrows that had missed their target. A potential problem with any of these dogs is that their instinct to enter water is so strong that they may plunge into a dirty canal or pond or even into rough seas. Keep your dog on the leash near dangerous waters and train him to react without delay to your instructions. However, members of this group are often powerful swimmers and can usually manage to escape danger.

Standard Poodle

Due mainly to its highly manicured appearance, many people are amazed that the standard poodle—the largest of today's three poodle breeds—was originally developed as a hunting dog. However, these dogs were prepared in this way to help them carry out their

Retrievers make excellent companions because of the way they interact with their owners. Their retrieving instincts are manifested today in pet dogs.

Breeds Needing Special Grooming

- Airedale terrier
- Keeshond
- Komonodor
- Old English sheepdog
- Maltese
- Poodle
- Portuguese water dog
- Puli

One of the distinctive features of the Irish water spaniel is its coloration. The one pictured above is chocolate, with a purplish hue evident in some lights, described officially as "puce liver."

task safely: The body was left covered with fur as insulation from the cold; the area around the leg joints was trimmed free of fur so the dog could move more freely when swimming; the top of the tail was shaped into a pom-pom so it could be tracked when swimming. Later small versions of the breed were created as companion rather than working dogs (see page 39).

Breeds Prone to Obesity

- Basset hound
- Bulldog
- Cairn terrier
- Cavalier King Charles spaniel
- Labrador retriever
- Golden retriever

Irish Water Spaniel

The Irish water spaniel is the tallest of all spaniels and particularly striking because of its very distinctive coat. The fur forms ringlets and is a unique shade of chocolate, described as "puce liver" because of its purplish hue. The coat has a slightly oily texture, which

repels water, so when the dog emerges onto land and shakes the water from his coat, it will dry off relatively quickly. Unfortunately, the origin of this particular breed is unclear, because its founder kept the details a closely guarded secret. However, the bloodline may have included poodles as well as the Portuguese water dog.

Portuguese Water Dog

This is a breed that traditionally accompanied fishermen along the Algarve coast. In the 1960s fewer than 50 of these amazing dogs survived, making it among the rarest breeds in the world. But thanks to a careful breeding program, their future is now more certain. The plume on the tail enables them to be spotted in the sea more easily.

Retrievers

True retrievers have a more recent ancestry— they were bred as sporting companions on the great estates of England in the 1800s, when shooting with guns became fashionable. However, the origins of these dogs actually lies in Canada. Lively and responsive, retrievers were bred to have considerable stamina, so they do not thrive in urban settings. They require

The golden retriever is a very popular breed today, being kept both as a working companion and as a pet. Its coat is noticeably longer than that of the Labrador retriever.

The Portuguese water dog was originally developed to work alongside fishermen. Not too long ago the breed was on the verge of extinction, but today its future is looking much more secure.

space and plenty of exercise. They tend to be quite greedy when it comes to food, so their diet needs to be controlled to prevent them from becoming overweight.

Labrador Retriever

The ancestors of the Labrador retriever were Canadian fishermen's dogs that were used to help haul in nets. This explains the breed's natural affiliation with water, a trait also associated with other members of the group.

Chesapeake Bay Retriever and Nova Scotia Duck-tolling Retriever

The Chesapeake Bay retriever and the Nova Scotia duck-tolling retriever are

also descended from Canadian dogs. The latter breed is credited with attracting waterfowl within reach of waiting guns by splashing its tail around in the water.

Flat-Coated and Curly Coated Retriever

The retriever's link with early water dogs is most clearly seen in the case of the curly coated retriever. The fur of this breed is tightly curled, although the hair on the face is smooth. These dogs are often liver-colored.

Further crosses led to the development of other types of retriever; the flat-coated retriever is the result of pairing the Labrador back to its Newfoundland ancestor—although this particular breed is kept more as a working gundog than as a companion.

Although Labrador retrievers come in several color variations, including black and chocolate, the yellow Labrador (not to be confused with the golden retriever) is the most common choice for a pet. Labrador retrievers are also popular sporting companions.

Hunting Dogs

Until the late 1800s, hunting was largely a way of obtaining food, but—perhaps confusingly—not all breeds that originally hunted are classified as hounds today; the term was applied only to breeds that actively pursued game throughout the countryside.

Several other groups of dog were developed as hunting companions as well, and their working skills are often still highly valued today. In fact, there are often both working and show strains, which have often diverged slightly—show dogs tend to have a more profuse coat than their working relatives, whose appearance is considered less significant. These breeds can be broadly divided into spaniels, setters, and pointers, each of which has its own distinctive style of working.

Spaniels

Like other gundogs, spaniels are very lively dogs. When out for a walk in the countryside, they often keep their nose close to the earth, seeking scents as they scurry along. Their eagerness is such that they may set off without heeding their owner's instructions, so effective training is very important from an early age—but this needs to be very positive to avoid repressing their natural enthusiasm.

Cocker spaniels were originally bred as hunting companions, which helps to explain their high level of energy. The breed's natural enthusiasm is one of the factors that appeals to many owners.

English Springer Spaniel

This is the original ancestor of most other British spaniel breeds. Its name refers to the way in which these gundogs work, with "spring" in this case meaning "to flush"—these dogs scurry through vegetation to drive out game, causing birds to take flight in front of waiting guns.

Spaniels make ideal companions because they are eager to please and they can form a strong bond with their owners.

English and American Cocker Spaniel

This slightly smaller gundog is a popular companion, partly because of its size. The breed was originally used to seek and flush out game birds called woodcock, which often hide away in undergrowth. The dogs retrieved any shot woodcock, returning them to the handler. Their broad nostrils are a sign of good scenting skills, and—as with many breeds working in this type of terrain—their ears hang down the sides of the head to protect the inner ear from sharp vegetation. The English form of the cocker spaniel was later refined into a slightly smaller American strain, which was employed in more open country in North America, primarily for hunting quails.

Other Spaniel Breeds

A number of other spaniel breeds are now very rare, such as the Clumber spaniel, which has a heavy, thickset appearance. Although not as fast as the cocker spaniel, this breed is known to be a dedicated worker in the field. Another less common spaniel is the Sussex, which is distinguished by its golden-liver coloration. Unusually, it bays like a scent hound when on a trail, perhaps providing a clue to its ancestry.

A number of other spaniel breeds originate from Europe. They include the French spaniel itself, whose origins date back to at least the 1600s, and the epagneul Picard, which arose in the area of Picardy. These breeds are usually seen only at shows in their area of origin and are rarely found as household pets, although they are loyal companions. These older breeds of French spaniel display an obvious relationship to setters in their overall appearance.

Family Dogs

- Labrador retriever
- American cocker spaniel
- Bichon frise
- Cavalier King Charles spaniel
- Miniature poodle
- Whippet
- Beagle

Don't be fooled by the appearance of a cocker spaniel puppy. Its coat, especially the fur on its ears, is much shorter than that of an adult dog. Grooming is very important for the cocker spaniel's well-being, partly to prevent them from developing ear infections.

English Setter

A traditional breed that is easily recognized by its mottled coloration, the English setter is not often seen today, particularly as a pet. It has a very responsive personality, however, and a wonderfully soft, silky coat. Even when the fur becomes muddy, the dog can be groomed without difficulty, because mud brushes out of the coat easily once it has dried.

Pointers

These breeds represent a further ancient division within the gundog category. Although stemming from a

Setters possess great stamina, with their ancestors having been kept as sporting companions over the course of centuries. Therefore, they must have plenty of exercise and are most content living in rural areas.

Sweet and affectionate, Irish setters are compatible with children and other dogs, but they need plenty of exercise and do not make ideal guard dogs.

Setters

The name comes from the way in which these dogs will set, or sit, to indicate the presence of game. Although active by nature, setters are less responsive to training than retrievers because, for example, they are more inclined to run off. They can, however, evolve into talented working dogs.

Irish (Red) Setter

Often mistakenly called the red setter because of its chestnut-red coloration, the Irish setter is the most popular member of this particular lineage of gundogs. Full of enthusiasm, the Irish setter is a breed that thrives in a home with active teenagers. It needs plenty of exercise off the leash, rather than a sedate walk around the local park.

Pointers are highly effective trackers, freezing in the characteristic "point," often with a front paw raised, when they locate their quarry.

common ancestor, pointers developed along slightly different lines depending on the European terrain over which they worked. Native breeds of pointer can be found in Spain, Portugal, France, Belgium, England, Germany, Denmark, the Czech Republic, and Italy. In some cases there are a number of regional variants as well. In France these range from the large French pointer, which originated in the Pyrenean region of the country, to smaller dogs, from Gascony, Auvergne, and Bourbon. Pointers are powerful dogs and quite determined by nature.

English Pointer

The most evident feature of the English pointer is its broad, concave muzzle. This is used to detect the scents of quarry, such as hares, wafted in minute amounts along air currents. The powerful build of the breed, including its muscular thighs, indicates its stamina.

The English pointer was first developed in the 1600s, and throughout the centuries its working instincts have become so well established that even a pet pointer will react by adopting its characteristic stance should it detect quarry when out for a walk.

German Pointer

There are smooth, long, and wire-haired forms of the German pointer, indicating an ability to hunt in different types of terrain. This intelligent breed is affectionate and not aggressive, but needs a lot of mental stimulation—for example, obedience and agility training.

Easy-to-Groom Dogs

- Beagle
- Basenji
- Boston terrier
- Dalmatian
- Hungarian vizsla
- Italian greyhound
- Manchester terrier
- Smooth-coated dachshund
- Staffordshire bull terrier
- Whippet

Other Hunting Dogs

There were also other hunting dogs that were used to help procure food, some of which are very specialized.

Hungarian Vizsla

This gundog is very versatile, able to both point and retrieve, and it has become more prominent over recent years—partly because of its striking looks. The name vizsla translates as "alert" or "responsive," indicating the characteristics of this breed, which have led to increasing popularity as a companion dog. As a pet, this breed is intelligent, affectionate, and loyal.

Norwegian Puffin Dog or Lundehund

This breed originated from islands lying within the Arctic Circle, where puffins come ashore to nest every spring. The fledgling puffins were hunted by dogs as they emerged after hatching in underground burrows on steep cliffs. This was dangerous work; moreover, throughout the centuries the appearance of the Lundehund became modified to assist them in their task.

The most obvious change is in their large paws, which have additional claws to help the dogs both hang on and clamber up the cliff face. Their forelegs became very flexible, while the neck displays an unusually

The Lundehund is one of the most specialized dog breeds in the world, although its working days are now a thing of the past.

A Hungarian Vizsla puppy. This breed can be trained quite easily and is intelligent, affectionate, and loyal. Its short coat is easy to groom, but there is also a rarer, rough-coated variety.

wide degree of movement, helping the Lundehund gain easier access to the puffins' burrows.

The hunting season was very brief, lasting just a few weeks in late summer, but the dogs instinctively knew what to do. They took the puffins back to their owners, who used the birds for meat and the feathers to fill pillows. This unique breed of dog might have died out in the late 1800s after hunters changed over to nets to collect young puffins, but breed enthusiasts managed to preserve the Lundehund and its unique features. Today the breed is common, both in its Norwegian homeland and elsewhere in the world, and is often acquired for its companionship.

Weimaraner

Its graceful movement and sleek coat make this an attractive breed. There are short-haired and long-haired varieties, but the long-haired is less common and is not accepted in the United States. Weimaraners are quick-witted, eager to please, and intelligent but can be dominant. Although they need regular exercise to avoid becoming destructive and unhappy, they make excellent guards.

The Weimaraner's distinctive color has made it a popular breed with dog owners worldwide.

Terriers

The British Isles is the main home of most breeds of terrier, although they are now found all over the world. Terriers were originally developed on farms to curb the spread of vermin, such as rats. Even though they are small, terriers are by no means lap dogs—they have very determined, bold natures and are not easily intimidated by larger dogs. A number of breeds were traditionally used by huntsmen to flush out foxes from underground.

Ever alert, terriers are very effective watchdogs, but they have an innate desire to dig, thanks to their background. This makes them a difficult prospect for gardeners, since they may excavate holes in the lawn and in flower beds on a regular basis. They are also not an ideal choice for families with young children, because they are not very tolerant of repeated handling. Terriers are generally hardy and quite robust, and their coats need relatively little attention, reflecting their outdoor nature. The breed does not usually shed fur, and in many cases the coat has a wiry texture; if so, it must be kept in shape by stripping. This should be done by a groomer, which adds to the cost of caring for these dogs. If you live in an area where there is a lot of space for your dog to exercise, you can be assured of a true companion.

British Terriers

Many terrier breeds are Scottish in origin, including the Cairn, the Skye, and the West Highland white.

Scottish Terrier

Scottish terriers are short-legged, compact, and sturdily built with a muscular neck. In temperament they are alert, quick, and feisty—perhaps

Famous terriers include Toto from *The Wizard of Oz* and Snowy from the Tintin series of children's stories.

even more so than other terrier breeds. Although very loving, they can also be stubborn and are prone to digging in the earth, as well as chasing and hunting small vermin.

Cairn Terrier
Short-legged and strongly built, the Cairn terrier has a hard coat—which needs weekly grooming—and small pointy ears. Cairns are bursting with energy and must be given plenty of time to run and play. They are cheerful, alert, lively, extrovert, and are excellent with children and other dogs.

Skye Terrier
Skye terriers are double-coated, with a short, soft undercoat and a hard, straight topcoat that is flat to the body without any curl. The coat is resistant

Dognosis
Scottish Breeds

There are five breeds of terrier that originated in Scotland: Scottish (or Aberdeen), Cairn, Dandie Dinmont, Skye, and West Highland white. They are all similar in temperament, with each being alert, intelligent, and playful. The oldest of the Scottish terriers is thought to be the Scottie, with the first reference to this dog matching a description dating from 1436. However, this is disputed because Scottish terriers were originally grouped together under the name Skye terriers. It wasn't until the 19th century and a growth in the popularity of dog shows that it was decided some distinction was necessary and the five separate breeds were thus established.

The Skye is a sturdy little terrier with a tangle-resistant coat. It displays the playfulness that is found in all terrier breeds but is nevertheless a one-man dog.

to tangling but needs to be brushed at least once a week. Skyes are not vicious, but they are very distrustful of strangers.

West Highland White Terrier
This breed is currently one of the most popular members of the British terrier group. It has a beautiful shaggy coat, button nose, and small, erect ears, giving it a cute and cuddly image. West Highlands are cheeky, confident, and affectionate but also alert and courageous, making them good guard dogs. They are also excellent playmates for children.

The Airedale
is the largest of all
the terrier breeds.

Popular Breeds of Terrier

- Airedale
- American Staffordshire
- American toy
- Bedlington
- Border
- Boston
- Bull
- Cairn
- Dandie Dinmont
- English toy
- Irish
- Irish wheaten
- Lakeland
- Manchester
- Miniature bull
- Norfolk
- Norwich
- Parson Jack Russell
- Patterdale
- Scottish
- Skye
- Smooth fox
- Staffordshire bull
- Welsh
- West Highland white
- Wire fox
- Yorkshire

Dandie Dinmont Terrier

The Dandie Dinmont terrier was created in England's Lake District. It is easily recognizable by its distinctive head, which has a beautiful silky topknot and ear feathering. This is a very sociable dog and will behave perfectly with other household pets as long as they are introduced at the puppy stage.

Airedale Terrier

The largest member of the British terrier group is the Airedale, which is named after its area of origin, near the River Aire, in the English county of Yorkshire. Airedales are active dogs and need a reasonable amount of exercise daily—preferably with some time spent playing games that require them to use their considerable intelligence.

Sealyham Terrier

The Sealyham terrier was first bred in Wales, which is also home to the Welsh terrier. Sealyhams are alert and fearless and will disappear for an afternoon's hunting given the opportunity, but they have a friendly disposition and make ideal housedogs. Like many other terriers, the Sealyham's coat needs a good deal of attention to keep it in good condition.

Irish Terriers

A number of terrier breeds also originate from Ireland, including the Irish terrier itself and the striking Kerry blue. Puppies of the latter are born with black coats, and it takes up to 18 months for the distinctive bluish

The wire fox terrier (above) has a dense, wiry topcoat. The Jack Russell (below right) has a coat that is mainly white with colored patches that may be rough or smooth.

gray coloration to develop. Others of Irish descent include the soft-coated wheaten terrier, which is thought to be the oldest of Ireland's terrier breeds, and the Glen of Imaal terrier.

Wire and Smooth Fox Terrier

In some cases—as with fox terriers—there are both wire and smooth-coated forms available. Both types are small, active, and lively, with a long, lean head and a short back. These dogs should have lots of exercise—they are full of energy and like nothing better than a long walk. They should be kept on a leash because they love to chase, and they will go after cats even if they are used to being around them in the home.

European and Australian Terriers

A number of terrier-type breeds have been created in mainland Europe. These include German breeds, such as the Affenpinscher, with its wiry coat; related breeds, such as the Brussels griffon; and small pinschers. The Australian terrier was created from a combination of various European terriers that early settlers brought over to Australia. Further crossings involving the Yorkshire terrier then gave rise to the Australian silky breed.

Australian Silky Terrier

The most decorative of the terriers are the Yorkshire and its relative, the Australian silky. The latter is named for its area of origin and the texture of its fur. Still, even these decorative terriers display hunting instincts should an opportunity present itself.

Guardians

Dogs bred as guardians have a darker side to their nature, and many are large dogs of mastiff stock. Dogs also vary in their sociability toward their own kind. Scent hounds, for example, represent one extreme, being bred to work together in packs hunting collectively; they display many of the behavioral characteristics of wolves. At the other end of the scale are breeds such as bull terriers, whose origins date back to the days when dogfighting was a popular spectator sport.

Bull Mastiffs

In the 1800s, when dangerous gangs of poachers began to plague the large estates of England, gamekeepers who had to confront them set out to develop a stronger companion than the placid English mastiff they had once relied upon. They crossed the mastiff with the traditional long-legged form of the bulldog that existed then—which was far removed in profile from the rather squat, small breed of today—and named the result the bull mastiff.

These large dogs were adept at locating and pursuing trespassers during night or day, and they retained the power of the original breeds, so they were still more than capable of keeping a man pinned to the ground. But the biggest difference was that

they worked silently and gave little warning of an impending pounce, which afforded them the element of surprise when tackling poachers. However, they were not especially vicious—they would simply restrain a man using their physical power rather than attack him.

Bull mastiffs are natural guardians and will not back down from a fight.

Guard Dogs

- Beauceron
- Bull mastiff
- Doberman
- Mastiff
- Neopolitan mastiff
- Rottweiler

The Staffordshire bull terrier is one of the most popular dog breeds in the United Kingdom.

Pit Bull Terrier

The American pit bull terrier has gained a fearsome reputation for aggression, both toward other dogs and also toward people—to the extent that ownership of this particular breed is restricted, if not outlawed, in some parts of the world.

Staffordshire Bull Terrier

Staffordshire bull terriers, developed in the English county for which they are named, are sometimes aggressive in their relationships with other dogs. Power-packed, thanks to their stocky muscular physique, they are not inclined to back down if challenged. As a result, it is especially important to be in control of these dogs at all times, because if your dog becomes involved in a fight with another dog, it could have serious consequences. Conflict is likely if a Staffie encounters another of its own kind or a similarly assertive breed. The American form of the Staffie has a similar temperament, too.

Working Dogs

Many dogs were bred originally for farmwork but, surprisingly, this sometimes demanded an aggressive side. Working dogs can be roughly categorized into flock protectors, shepherd dogs, and collies. Both flock protectors and shepherd dogs are often referred to as sheepdogs.

Flock Protectors

When packs of wolves presented a serious threat to sheep and goats throughout much of Europe, dog breeds were developed to fight off predators. Such dogs often had white coats, which enabled them to merge with the flock without upsetting the sheep. They often wore spiked collars for their own protection in the event of an attack.

Anatolian Shepherd

In Turkey the Anatolian shepherd dog was bred to protect flocks. It is a muscular breed, with thick neck, broad head, and sturdy body. It was developed to be independent and forceful, responsible for guarding flocks alone, which makes it challenging as a pet.

Maremma

This breed is from Italy, and although fairly common there, it is very rare elsewhere. Maremmas are large, sturdy dogs, difficult to train, and

very strong-willed. They can handle a great deal of exercise, but it is not essential.

Pyrenean Mountain Dog

The Pyrenean mountain dog arose in the border area between France and Spain. After generations of selective breeding, the result is a kind-natured and gentle dog that for its size does not need copious amounts of exercise.

Above: As a flock guardian, the great Pyrenees or Pyrenean mountain dog used to wear a special metal collar with iron spikes to protect him when battling wolves.

Left: The Maremma sheepdog is a strong breed with a rather independent nature, reflecting its working past. It used to roam freely among flocks, protecting them from wolves. These dogs were not trained to heed instructions but instead to rely on their own initiative.

Komondors have a very distinctive coat that resembles dreadlocks and develops when the dog is around a year old.

Komondor

On farms across the plains of Hungary, the strong komondor carried out the protective role. An intelligent working animal capable of making decisions, the komondor retains its instinct to guard and protect even today. In temperament it is faithful and devoted, intensely loyal, and enjoys attention and close physical contact.

Pure black coloration is characteristic of this Belgian shepherd, which is also known as the Groenendael. It is of a lighter build than the German shepherd.

Shepherds

Working alongside the powerful flock guardians were smaller sheepdogs, whose task was to herd the livestock as required, with different breeds arising in different areas. While flock guardians differ significantly in appearance, various shepherds clearly have a common ancestry. Apart from the fact that they occur in a range of coat types, all these shepherds are similar: They have erect, triangular ears, which give them a rather lupine appearance, along with a very loyal, intelligent, and responsive temperament. As well as herding sheep over the past century, they have been used for a variety of other tasks, including serving as police dogs and in the armed services. They have also been trained to help the disabled.

German Shepherd

Of the European shepherds, the German form is by far the best known. This is a highly intelligent breed, and German shepherds need a great deal of mental stimulation. Young puppies should be exercised cautiously to avoid long-term damage to developing joints, but older dogs require long walks.

Belgian Shepherd/Groenendael/Teruveren/Malinois/Lakenois

Within Belgium there is a group of very similar breeds, occurring in different parts of the country, with a slightly lighter build than their German counterpart. They include

Belgian shepherd breeds are descended from the same ancestral stock and have evolved on separate lines in different parts of the country. They include the Malinois (left) and the Lakenois (below).

the black long-coated Groenendael and its close relative, the black-and-tan Teruveren, as well as the short-coated Malinois and the rare Lakenois, which is distinguished by its curly coat. Even less commonly seen internationally is the Dutch shepherd, which also occurs in three coat types and is thought to be descended from the Groenendael.

Briard
This is a medium-sized rugged, agile dog with a harsh coat. The briard is a very loyal breed, and after bonding with family members, it will be very protective—although it can be aloof with strangers.

Ten Things That Stress Your Dog

Some dogs are instinctively nervous, especially if they came from a shelter. Although many things can cause stress, here are a few of the more well known.

1. Fireworks
2. Thunderstorms
3. Other dogs
4. Boredom
5. Cats
6. Being teased while locked in a car
7. Visitors
8. Delayed mealtimes
9. A disrupted walking schedule
10. Being left alone for long periods

The briard is an affectionate and easily trained breed, with double dewclaws on its hind feet. Its coat feels very dry to the touch and protects the dog well against the elements.

Collies

These British breeds are ideally suited to working with sheep. Although collies are readily trainable, they are also instinctively active dogs, bred to work, so they will not settle well in the confines of a home. If left alone for long periods on a regular basis, they soon become destructive.

Border Collie

The border collie comes from the area between Scotland and England. These dogs must have plenty of exercise to keep them well muscled and their brains occupied or they will misbehave and become aggressive. Their coat is easy to maintain, providing they are brushed once a week and tangles are dealt with on a regular basis.

Rough and Smooth Collie

The rough and smooth collies originate from farther north than the border collie, in Scotland itself. The rough collie has a long, heavy coat to cope with the harsh weather in the Scottish Highlands, while the smooth collie adopted a shorter coat more suited to the milder lowlands. Both

breeds are friendly, never aggressive, and enjoy lots of exercise.

Cattle Dogs

Other dogs have been bred to work with cattle rather than sheep, which often require more active persuasion to encourage them to move. Strange as it may seem, many types of cattle dog are small and short-legged so they can move easily between the cattle's feet and avoid painful blows from hooves. At the same time, the dogs are able to nip the backs of the cow's feet if necessary, encouraging a reluctant animal to move forward.

Corgis

The Cardigan and Pembroke Welsh corgis are now generally recognized as two separate breeds, although the division has only recently been officially delineated for show purposes. The Cardigan can be distinguished by its larger ears and long tail.

Swedish Vallhund

Both these corgi breeds bear a remarkable resemblance to the Swedish vallhund, which has become better known internationally. None of these breeds is an ideal choice as a pet in a household with young children, because they are not especially patient and will not hesitate to nip if frustrated, just as if they were working.

The Swedish vallhund has a remarkably similar appearance to the Welsh corgi, despite there being no apparent direct ancestral link.

Lancashire Heeler

Arising in the north of England, this breed bears a striking similarity to corgis, both in its appearance and temperament. It was developed from matings between corgis and the local Manchester terrier—notably around

A litter of Border collie pups with their parents. These sheepdogs are considered to be one of the most intelligent of all breeds; unfortunately, they are not well suited to being kept as pets, because they can easily become bored in the home.

To withstand the rigors of the outback, the Australian cattle dog was bred for good overall health, strength, and an easy-to-care-for coat.

A Dog's Tale
The Oldest-Living Dog

An Australian cattle dog called Bluey currently holds the record for canine longevity. He worked on a farmstead in Queensland, Australia, and lived for 29 human years.

the village of Ormskirk, which is why the breed also became known as the Ormskirk terrier. These dogs display the characteristic behaviors of both ancestors, being valued not only for herding cattle but also for hunting vermin, in true terrier tradition.

Australian Cattle Dog

A tough breed with considerable stamina was required by Australian farmers to work their cattle. They needed to be able to keep up and work alongside the horses used for herding on vast farmsteads. As a result, the Australian cattle dog differs in appearance from the short-legged British breeds. A variety of breeds was involved in its ancestry, including the dalmatian (see page 48), which is known for its stamina. The

dalmatian's influence is still seen in Australian cattle dog puppies, which are white at birth.

Crosses with the feral dingo also aided the development of these dogs, helping them to work silently without panicking the cattle, although they operate in a similar way to corgis, nipping at the animals' heels. There is a second variety, called the stumpy-tailed cattle dog, or Smithfield heeler, which can easily be distinguished by its short tail.

American Cattle Dogs

In the United States there are a number of localized cattle dog breeds, but they tend not to be seen in the show ring. As with several other American hound breeds, such as the Plott hound, many of these dogs are named after their original creators. A typical example is the blue Lacy—named for the four Lacy brothers, who took their dogs with them when they drove their cattle from Kentucky to Texas. The blue Lacy in turn is closely related to the Catahoula leopard dog, which is especially valued for rounding up cattle that have been roaming free.

Such breeds are still kept as farm dogs, proving both friendly companions and dedicated workers. However, they are rarely seen outside their area of origin, because they are not suited to living in urban surroundings. Their working instincts also mean that in rural areas they need to be well trained to ensure they do not interfere with stock when taken out for a walk.

Draft Dogs

In some parts of the world, the dog has been a vital lifeline. High in the Swiss Alps, for centuries before roads were built, draft dogs were used to take local processed foods—such as alpine cheese—to market. These dogs needed to be strong, yet also very dependable and placid, and they usually worked together in pairs.

Swiss Mountain Dog

The largest of these draft breeds is the greater Swiss mountain dog, which has a smooth coat. However, the longer-coated Bernese mountain dog tends to be better known among canine enthusiasts today.

Both display similar patterning—mainly black, with chestnut coloring on the legs, a white blaze on the face extending down to the chest, and white paws, creating an attractive appearance.

Alaskan Malamute

Dogs also once provided the only means of transport through much of the Arctic region, and they are still used for this purpose today. The breed name of these dogs frequently reflects that of the tribe with which it is associated. An example of this is the Alaskan malamute, believed to be one of the oldest members of this group of spitz breeds. Originating from the far North, these dogs are distinguished by their pricked ears and a tail that curls forward over their back. In the winter they were harnessed together in teams to pull sleds, while during the summer they carried individual loads in packs hung over the sides of their bodies. The packs could weigh up to 50 lb. (23 kg), but the dogs are capable of covering distances of about 20 miles (32 km) a day.

Siberian Husky

Other sled dogs are of a lighter build and faster on the move, such as the Siberian husky, whose name is based on the Chukchi tribe, who live in far northeast Siberia. The

Striking pale blue eyes are often a feature of the Siberian husky, and it is by no means unusual to come across a Siberian husky with one blue and one brown or hazel eye. The patterning of these dogs is highly individual, enabling them to be distinguished easily, even from some distance away.

Chocolate coloration is not uncommon in the case of the Alaskan malamute— one of the most powerful of all sled breeds.

A Dog's Tale
Husky Help

In 1925 the speed and tenacity of the Siberian husky once helped to prevent a major outbreak of diphtheria in the Alaskan city of Nome. Blizzard conditions meant that a team of huskies, under the control of musher Leonhard Seppala, offered the only hope of delivering the antiserum. They got through, saving many lives, and a statue commemorating this event was erected in Central Park, New York, where it can still be seen today.

remoteness of this area means that these dogs have remained purebred for perhaps longer than almost any other breed, over 3,000 years. One indication of this is in the way these huskies howl like wolves instead of barking.

Although many sled dogs can be rather quarrelsome with one another, Siberian huskies were reared to ensure they are tolerant and well adjusted. The women cared for the dogs when they were not working, so children played with them, and only the relatively placid animals were kept for breeding.

Samoyed

One of the most distinctive of the spitz breeds is the Samoyed, named after the Samoyede people of northern Siberia. This breed is

now characterized by its luxuriant snow-white coat, although in its homeland it once occurred in other colors, including both sable and black and white. In Siberia this breed was traditionally more widely used for herding livestock than hauling

The beautiful snow-white appearance of the Samoyed (right) belies a tough and very hardy dog, bred to survive under extreme conditions.

loads, but it came to prominence in the West as a sled dog. Captain Robert F. Scott and others took Samoyeds on a number of expeditions to the South Pole. The breed has a stubborn streak—as do most sled dogs—and needs plenty of human contact to avoid becoming bored.

Japanese Spitz Breeds

As members of the spitz group were taken farther south, they became smaller in size. In many cases they ended up as companion breeds in Europe—as reflected by the German spitz breeds, the smallest of which is the pomeranian. During the 20th century this bloodline in turn led to the creation of American Eskimo bloodlines by dog show aficionados in the United States.

Akita

It is in Japan, however, that the spitz breeds had their greatest impact and the majority of Japanese native breeds are descended from stock of this type. The largest example is the akita, which was developed as a fighting dog on the main island of Honshu in the 1600s. Not surprisingly, members of this particular breed are often not friendly toward other dogs.

Ainu

Other Japanese spitz breeds are smaller in size and more docile, such as the Ainu, bred as a hunter, companion, and guardian and named after the people who introduced it to

Japan thousands of years ago. The kai dog is another hunting breed, classed as a shika inu, which means "medium-sized dog," along with the similar Kishu (Kyushu) dog. The rarest of this group of spitz dogs is the Shikoku shika inu, from the Kochi region of Japan. The shiba inu, or "small dog," is the most popular companion breed, although it is also used to hunt birds.

Japanese Spitz

A much more recent addition to this group is the Japanese spitz itself. These dogs are pure white, resembling a tiny Samoyed since they stand about 12 inches (30 cm) tall. They may be partly descended from the Samoyed, having come to prominence during the 20th century.

The akita is a powerful breed with a dominant nature. Male puppies grow slightly larger than bitches. These dogs have a reputation for displaying great loyalty toward their owners but need strict training.

Rural Dogs

- Alaskan malamute
- Bloodhound
- Great Dane
- Irish wolfhound
- Otterhound
- Pyrenean mountain dog
- St. Bernard

Other Working Dogs

A number of these were developed to perform very specific tasks, such as running alongside horse-drawn carriages or accompanying riders on horseback to protect against attack by highwaymen. Others were evolved to act as bedwarmers, although most members of the group were created primarily as guardians.

Dalmatian

Dalmatians have almost boundless energy because they were originally bred as carriage dogs. Dalmatians still retain their natural athleticism and must have plenty of exercise to prevent them from becoming bored, particularly when left alone. Despite the name, the breed's origins are unclear, and there are no firm links to

The spotted patterning of these young dalmatians will not change as they grow older, being virtually as distinctive as our fingerprints.

the Dalmatian coast. This is a very popular breed today, partly because of its striking and highly individual black-spotted patterning. Puppies are pure white at birth and only start to develop their individual spotting at about three weeks old.

Hairless Dogs

A most unusual characteristic of some breeds of dog is the absence of hair. There are several breeds that display this trait, and the gene that causes lack of hair seems to have emerged both in China and in Middle America. It may also result in missing teeth. Such dogs are highly controversial—people either love them or hate them. They are not totally hairless; they retain a slight covering of fur—especially on the extremities of the body, such as the ears, tail, and feet.

Chinese Crested Breed

This breed gets its name from the fur on the top of the head, creating what appears to be a crest. The dogs' skin feels quite warm, but it needs protection—both against the cold and also with a special canine sunblock to prevent sunburn. Like other similar breeds from around the world, the Chinese crested has a friendly nature, having been kept as a companion for centuries. Litters normally have a mixture of hairless puppies and those with a normal covering of hair, known as powder puffs.

Mexican Hairless Dog or Xoloitzcuintli

Middle America has the greatest diversity of hairless breeds—although a number documented by early explorers now appear to be extinct. However, there are still three separate sizes of the Mexican hairless dog, or xoloitzcuintli, but the toy form is a modern creation dating back to the 1950s.

Peruvian Inca Orchid

The other two surviving hairless dogs are found in Peru. There is a dark form, as well as the pale-skinned, dark-spotted Peruvian Inca orchid. This latter breed was also known as the moonflower dog, because it was only allowed out at night due to its pale skin.

These Middle American dogs were originally viewed as a source

of food, but gradually they became predominantly used as bedwarmers. These days they can be very protective in domestic surroundings, especially if strangers are visiting the home.

How It Feels

The texture of a dog's fur varies significantly between breeds. This is a reflection of the proportions of different types of hair present in the coat. Here are some typical coat textures:

Coat texture	Breed
Soft	Smooth-coated dachshund (see page 22).
Bouncy	Irish water spaniel (see page 24).
Harsh and wiry	Airedale terrier (see page 35).
Raised, slightly wavy coat	Maremma sheepdog (see page 39).
Long and silky	Pekingese (see page 54).
Similar to the skin of a peach	Hairless breeds (see page 48).
Similar to cotton	Coton de Tulear (see page 51).

The Chinese crested breed occurs in two forms—this is the so-called hairless variety, which has long hair only on its extremities, in contrast to the powder puff, which has a normal coat.

Small Dogs

While some dog breeds are defined by their origins, others are essentially categorized by their small size. The temperament of these breeds is much more variable, depending on their origins. The ancestry of many small dogs can be traced back to the royal courts of Europe, where it was once fashionable to create miniature versions of hunting dogs as pets for ladies of the court.

Italian Greyhound
The earliest breed created in this way was the Italian greyhound, a scaled-down miniature version of the larger breed. Dogs of this type appear in portraits of European nobility from the 1400s onward, but the breed's origins may even extend back to ancient Egypt. Their temperament is very similar to that of their larger relatives.

Miniature and Toy Poodle
Some attempts at miniaturization are much more recent, however. Originally there was only the standard poodle, but its popularity in the early years of the 20th century led to the development of a smaller breed: the miniature poodle. Subsequently, an even smaller variant was created in the United States—the toy poodle. These dogs are simply scaled-down versions of their larger relative—the toy poodle stands just 10 inches (25 cm) high, while the standard version measures 15 inches (38 cm) at the shoulder.

Pugs rank among the most distinctive of all toy dogs. They make lovable, friendly companions, but they do have a tendency to snore, due to their compact facial shape.

City Dogs

- Chihuahua
- Japanese chin
- Pekingese
- Pomeranian
- Pug
- Shih tzu
- Toy poodle

Big or Small?

The wide range in the size of domestic dog breeds is due to their ancestor. In the past, gray wolves varied even more significantly in size than the populations that exist today—the largest examples of the species occur in the far north of North America, but there was once a race of gray wolves that stood just 12 inches (30 cm) high.

Unfortunately, these small wolves, described as shamanu (*Canis lupus hodophilax*), were hunted out of existence early in the 20th century. However, it is apparent that a wide range in size was natural in the case of the gray wolf, so its canine descendants also appear in different sizes.

Bichon Frise

Where these dogs originated remains a mystery, but there are now a number of breeds that are descended from them, and they are often described as being of bichon stock. The best-known example of this group of toy breeds is the bichon frise itself, which was popular in the royal courts of Europe.

Coton de Tulear

Other examples include the exotic and rare Coton de Tulear, from the island of Madagascar, and a similar breed, from the nearby island of Reunion,

The bichon frise is a friendly and very adaptable dog, having been kept both as a favored companion of royalty and also as a talented circus performer.

The coats of puppies often differ significantly from those of adult dogs, being significantly shorter, as shown by this young poodle.

Maltese

Rather than being simply a scaled-down version of an existing breed, the Maltese is perhaps the most ancient lineage of small dogs. As its name suggests, the breed is closely linked to the Mediterranean island of Malta. The Phoenicians, a seafaring people from present-day North Africa who traded widely around the Mediterranean and farther afield, may have been responsible for taking the Maltese to other areas. They were kept as companions, being highly sought after by wealthy families in ancient Greece.

The Coton de Tulear is so-called because of its fluffy white coat, which both looks and feels rather like cotton. It is now becoming increasingly well known both in North America and Europe.

Below right: Pomeranians are significantly scaled down in size from their larger German spitz relatives.

which is now extinct. Both these breeds are thought to have descended from bichon stock brought from Europe by French settlers in the 1600s. Having been kept as a companion for centuries, the Coton de Tulear excels in this role, being very friendly and loyal by nature. Its coat is soft, like cotton in texture, and often white although bi- and tricolored variants are also known.

Havanese

In the United States the bichon is represented by the Havanese, named after Cuba's capital. Although these breeds do differ slightly in appearance after being isolated over the course of centuries, their underlying temperaments are all very similar: playful and affectionate.

King Charles or Toy Spaniel

Some of the most popular breeds today are the toy spaniels, particularly the English toy spaniel, known as the King Charles Spaniel in England, where it originated. These small dogs were a particular favorite of King Charles II; he used to exercise them himself in London. However, over the course of the centuries, their appearance changed; they developed much shorter noses than their ancestors, as seen in contemporary

A Dog's Tale
The Impact of Miniaturization

Reducing the size of some breeds has led to a wide range of health problems, such as patellar luxation, which affects the kneecaps and may require corrective surgery. However, the trend is to produce ever smaller dogs, which are often referred to as teacup breeds because of their very small size. Such dogs are created by selecting the smallest of breeds—such as the Yorkshire terrier—then pairing them to create even smaller dogs. This approach is not always successful, however, because some puppies in the litter are likely to be larger than others.

portraits. This encouraged a wealthy American, Roswell Eldridge, to offer large cash prizes at Cruft's Dog Show in the 1920s for spaniels that were similar in type to those seen in London nearly 300 years previously.

As these "original" spaniels were re-created, their popularity overtook that of the contemporary breed, and they are now the most popular companion breed. They have an attractive appearance and a friendly, enthusiastic personality, but they are prone to a number of health issues. Heart problems are of particular concern. This may be due to the relatively small number of dogs used to create the breed. It is important to have puppies checked at an early stage for any apparent defects, and you must not allow these spaniels to become overweight; they are very susceptible to obesity, and this will exacerbate any cardiac problem.

Pomeranian

The breed that occurs in the greatest number of sizes is the German spitz, the smallest variety of which is the Pomeranian, named for the German state where it was created. The range in size is not great: The giant form measures about 16 inches (41 cm) at the shoulder, with the Pomeranian itself standing just 5 inches (12.5 cm) shorter. All scaled-down breeds have a temperament similar to their bigger relatives, so Pomeranians are lively and alert guardians.

A young Cavalier King Charles spaniel. It is important that puppies are checked by a veterinarian for possible congenital heart problems and patellar luxation, to which they are susceptible.

Despite its name, the Tibetan spaniel is not a true spaniel. Its origins lie in the Far East. It is very affectionate and has plenty of energy. This may be a reflection of the fact that in its homeland it was employed by monks to turn their prayer wheels by trotting from spoke to spoke inside them.

The Pekingese's round and shortened face is very clearly apparent in profile.

Pekingese and Tibetan Spaniel

A number of small companion dogs originated from China and its neighboring countries, where they were kept for many centuries before they became known in Europe. The Pekingese is probably the best-known member of this group. It was once called a sleeve dog because it could be concealed within the flowing robes of Chinese courtiers and was considered so precious that stealing one was punishable by execution.

The Tibetan spaniel is a close relative of the Pekingese, although their relationship today is less obvious because through the 20th century selective breeding has altered the appearance of the Pekingese. Its face has become much more rounded and compact compared with the appearance of the original Pekingese brought to Britain, whose facial features were more similar to those of its Tibetan relative.

Although selective breeding does not alter a breed's temperament, it may have an influence on its behavior. In the case of the Pekingese, for instance, the reduction in the length of the nose has made the breed more susceptible to heat stroke in hot weather, while the eyes have become more prominent, making them more susceptible to injury. These dogs also tend to snore when they are asleep.

Like many small dogs, both these breeds make formidable watchdogs, barking loudly when there are strangers around. This reflects their ancestry—larger dogs patrolled outside, but if a would-be thief or assassin eluded them, the smaller dog inside made a noise to indicate there was an intruder on the premises.

Designer Dogs

A new trend that has emerged over recent years is the development of "designer dogs"—breeds that are developed purely for their looks rather than for their working abilities. Well over a hundred such crosses have already been carried out, but they represent only a tiny percentage of possible crosses, since there are so many breeds in existence worldwide. Some of these new breeds are the result of random mating, which led to the appearance of cute puppies, but in other cases mating is carried out to combine desirable characteristics from both breeds.

Pairing existing breeds to develop new forms has been done in the cat world for many years but is a relatively new phenomenon as far as dogs are concerned. The resulting puppies often vary widely in appearance, with some resembling one parent more than the other—unlike true breeds, they are not standardized in appearance, because this can only be achieved over numerous generations. It is no coincidence that poodles generally play a prominent part in the creation of these new breeds. Poodles are an ancient lineage of dogs used to working closely alongside people, and they are highly trainable, with some having performed in circus rings.

Changing Fashions

The popularity of different breeds changes over the years—this is reflected by the annual figures published by the various kennel clubs, which reveal how many puppies of each breed have been registered. The Labrador retriever has now become the most numerous breed of dog worldwide, partly due to its attractive looks and ease of grooming, and partly to its enthusiastic nature.

Another trend over recent years has been a move toward smaller dogs, with the popularity of the Chihuahua, in particular, having increased. Small dogs fit well with contemporary lifestyles, where lack of space often precludes keeping a large dog and the opportunity for exercise is limited to city parks.

Some traditional working breeds, such as the otterhound and working terriers, have faded in popularity—largely as a result of their active temperament, which means they do not adapt well to living in urban areas. The way dogs are portrayed in the media can also have an effect: The appearance of a breed in the company of a well-known personality, or in a popular film, can have a dramatic impact on the number of people interested in acquiring a dog of that type.

Their curly coated appearance is very distinctive, and because they exist in three sizes, they can be crossed with a variety of different dogs. Established designer dogs generally do develop set characteristics intermediate between those of their constituent breeds, and their temperament is also likely to be intermediate following an initial cross of this type, even if their appearance differs.

There will be many other crosses of this type carried out in the future, and new breeds will emerge. This is a reflection of our changing lifestyles; whereas the choice of a dog used to be determined largely by the work he did, other factors have now become more significant, and the emphasis today is more on the way that he looks. Most people consider appearance the critical factor when choosing a dog rather than the dog's temperament—which stems from its ancestry. However, by using highly trainable dogs in the breeding of designer dogs, it is possible to create new types of dogs with both friendly natures and an attractive appearance. As an example, hounds such as the various bassets have short legs, enabling accompanying huntsmen to keep up with them on foot, but they are difficult to train. By crossing a basset with a poodle, it may be possible to retain the appealing characteristics of the bassett—such as its long, pendulous ears and short legs—but create a more obedient and less energetic offspring.

Labradoodle

A few designer dogs have become established as new breeds; the best-known example is probably the labradoodle, bred from crosses between Labrador retrievers and standard poodles. Its origins date back to the 1960s.

Kyi Leo or American Lamalese

About 20 years earlier, in the San Jose area of California, a bloodline was created based on crosses of the Maltese and Lhasa apso breeds. These dogs were originally called Lhasa apso Maltese shaggies— reflecting both their origins and appearance, and they grew in popularity. In 1972 their name was changed to kyi leo, literally meaning "dog lion," although some breeders prefer the name American Lamalese.

A curly coat is associated with a number of breeds, such as the Welsh terrier shown here, and this characteristic is now being seen increasingly in designer dog bloodlines too, as reflected by the Labradoodle.

Labradoodles, such as this one, were created originally by crossbreeding and are now evolving into a new standardized breed. Labradoodles mated together will tend to produce puppies that resemble themselves in appearance.

Bond with Your Dog

A dog may be man's best friend, but understanding a few basic facts about your new pet will deepen your relationship. It is easier to bond with a young puppy; you can establish a routine that suits both of you from the beginning rather than trying to teach an older dog new tricks. But there are also a few things you must be aware of when introducing your new companion to other members of your household.

Deciding On a New Puppy

Puppies are born deaf and blind and gradually develop their senses as they grow older, but this does not mean they are cut off from the world around them and unable to function. Dogs just a few hours old will huddle together with their littermates to keep warm and separate if they start to become too hot. Once they are about two weeks old, their eyes open; in just one more week they will start to hear. They start to gain their milk teeth at this stage and begin the weaning process as they start to take solid food.

Puppies become increasingly mobile from this point on, which marks a significant phase in their development, often described as the socialization period. This is when a young dog starts to focus on the world around him. It begins at a month old and lasts until around 12 weeks, extending beyond the stage at which a puppy can be moved to a new home. This period shapes the puppy's future development and has a direct influence on his future relationships with people, so it is vital that during this time he becomes familiar with humans. If shut away in a kennel in relative isolation, a young dog is likely to become nervous of human contact, which will make it much harder for you to gain his confidence.

Not surprisingly, puppies that have been reared in the home are better able to socialize and are far more comfortable settling into new surroundings than those that have previously been kept in kennels, where there is minimal contact with people. For this reason it is wiser to acquire your puppy from a breeder who rears litters in the home. It is usually possible to check this, because breeders frequently advertise puppies

Dognosis Boy or Girl?

A male and a bitch are different in temperament, although this is unlikely to be apparent when they are puppies. Male dogs become more dominant, making training more difficult. They tend to grow larger than bitches and are more territorial, using their urine as a scent marker around the home. Male dogs are more likely to stray in search of a mate; females usually stray twice a year when in heat. Neutering from about six months old should prevent most problems; in males the surgery lowers testosterone levels and is done externally. In females it's invasive, so don't encourage exertion for a few weeks afterward. Surgery also protects her from pyometra, a potentially fatal condition affecting the reproductive tract. Both sexes are prone to putting on weight after neutering, due to hormonal changes, so regular weight checks are a good idea.

long before they are old enough to be transferred to a new home, and they welcome visits at this stage.

Consequently, you will be able to see firsthand how the bitch cares for the puppies and also to discover their living conditions. If you decide on one right then and there, it would be wise to photograph the puppy, particularly if he has individual markings, so there is no risk of your taking home a different member of the litter when the time comes—after he is fully weaned—usually at about eight to nine weeks old. Once you are certain that this is the right puppy for you, the breeder will most likely ask that you sign a contract and leave a deposit, so be sure to obtain a receipt before you leave.

Bringing Your Puppy Home

When you arrive home with your puppy, bear in mind that this will be the first time in his life that he will have been away from his littermates and mother. He may not show obvious signs of distress initially, because he will be excited to explore a new environment, but difficulty often occurs at night when the litter would be settling down to sleep together. If left on his own, your puppy will most likely start howling. It may help if you encourage him to play with you beforehand so that he will be more inclined to fall asleep, but this alone may not be the solution to obtaining

Starting out with a puppy means that it should be relatively easy to build a close bond between you, whereas adult dogs may be less trusting, particularly if they have been mistreated previously.

A dog soon comes to recognize the sound of his name if you use it whenever you are addressing your pet.

a good night's sleep. Also ensure that the temperature in the room where your new puppy is sleeping is relatively warm; if he feels cold, he is likely to wake up and then he may begin howling because he is feeling distressed being on his own.

Ultimately, your puppy will settle down and go back to sleep—if you try to comfort him, he will probably start howling again when you leave. Worse still, you may find that he will persist in behaving this way in the future rather than growing out of it, because it guarantees your attention. Further long-term problems will arise should your resolve weaken to the extent that you allow him to sleep in your bedroom. While a great Dane puppy, for example, may not occupy that much space, having an adult of this giant breed crashing on your bed each night is another matter entirely—and separation at this later stage is likely to be much more difficult. There is also the risk that your pet could introduce fleas or other parasites into your bedroom. If you try shutting your dog elsewhere in the home once he is approaching adulthood, not only is he

Dognosis
What's That Smell?

When cleaning up an accident, it is important to remove all tracks of the scent; otherwise, your puppy may return to the same spot again and again. Dogs use urine as a scent marker—in the wild, wolves mark the borders of their territory in this way in order to emphasize their presence—therefore, if the scent is still present, your pet will be attracted back. Certain disinfectants, especially pine-based products, are likely to reinforce rather than remove the scent, so it is better to rely on proprietary pet products that have been specially formulated for this purpose.

likely to bark but he may also scratch the door, damaging any woodwork. Be hard-hearted for a few nights at the beginning; your puppy will soon get used to being on his own and will sleep quite happily in his bed.

Cleanliness

Many people choose the kitchen as the location for their pet's bed because hard flooring is much easier to clean if there happens to be an accident. However, if you are attentive to your new pet's needs, there should be few, if any, accidents. Puppies are instinctively clean by nature, so if you place your pet outdoors first thing in the morning, then after each meal during the day and last thing at night, it should be easy to develop a routine. These are

What's in a Name?

One of the best ways to build a bond with your puppy is to select a name. If the breeder has given your puppy a name you do not like, you can change it at this early stage if you must, but use your pet's new name at every opportunity so he learns to recognize it and respond. It is harder with an older dog—once a dog has learned to respond to a name, it can be very difficult to change it without causing confusion in your pet's mind. It is very important that your puppy learns to respond to a name because—like much of the bonding in the early days at home—it will help to cement the relationship between you. It will also prove invaluable when you are away from the home environment, because your puppy will see you as his pack leader and instinctively be more inclined to return to you.

the stages when your puppy is most likely to want to relieve himself.

If you occasionally have to leave your puppy for a while and he will need to relieve himself in your absence, place him in an area that is easy to clean up. You can buy special pads to put down, or spread out some sheets of newspaper in the corner of the room—away from the sleeping area if your puppy is running free—or in his crate. These can be disposed of and the soiled floor area disinfected easily on your return.

Be patient with your puppy. If he does soil indoors, you probably failed to put him outside when he needed to go. There is absolutely no point in rubbing your pet's nose in the soiled area as a deterrent; he will not understand what he has done wrong.

If your pet persistently soils indoors, speak to your vet, because an underlying medical problem may be responsible. It could be a congenital problem affecting the urinary tract or, if his toilet training suddenly lapses, an infection might be the cause.

Puppies soon learn to relieve themselves outdoors in a specific place. Try to discourage your puppy from relieving himself on the lawn, because the acid in the urine will eventually kill the grass and you will begin to see patches throughout the yard where he has gone before. Instead, designate an area of pavement, mulch, or dirt. If your puppy wanders away from the area of the yard that you have set aside, there are sprays that should attract him back.

Picking Up Your Puppy

Another lesson a puppy needs to learn is to allow himself to be picked up without struggling. Although some breeds will grow too large to be carried, it is still useful to teach puppies that they have nothing to fear from this experience—you may someday need to lift your pet once he is fully grown, perhaps when you are bathing or grooming him. Being able to lift your dog without a struggle is especially important with dachshunds, because their long back means they are very susceptible to slipped intervertebral disks. They should never be asked to jump up or down when getting into and out of a car;

It can sometimes be very difficult to choose a puppy from a litter. As well as temperament, look for coloration, markings, or other characteristics that may draw you to an individual.

they should be carried if you do not have a special access ramp. It is also safer to carry them up and down stairs, and they should never be encouraged to jump alongside you onto a chair.

Picking up a puppy is relatively straightforward, but since they are quite excitable, young dogs often struggle, so you need to be careful that your pet does not slip out of your hands and fall. If you are right-handed, start by putting your left hand in front of your puppy's chest to restrain him, and then place your right hand under his chest, between the forelegs. Use your hands the other way around if you are left-handed. Lift up your

puppy, tucking his body against the side of yours to provide more support and also to prevent him from struggling. Most puppies are quite happy about being lifted up because it brings them closer to your face, which they may try to lick. Once you have picked up your puppy, walk around with him for a short time, then put him down and pick him up again. Repeat this regularly and your pet will readily accept being picked up and carried throughout his life.

Troubleshooting

There will be times when you need to stop your puppy from behaving in a certain way. To communicate this message effectively, you must be consistent—it is not fair to allow your puppy to sit on a sofa at times and then scold him for sleeping there on his own. He will not understand what is wrong.

Problems with puppies often seem to appear at around five months of age—to the extent that you may feel that your efforts at training your pet are beginning to fail. In particular, you will probably find that your puppy is gnawing more than ever—and not necessarily just on objects such as shoes, but also on chair legs or carpeting. There is good reason for this: Your pet will be teething and has an instinctive desire to chew to ease the pain. You need to be tolerant because this stage will pass, but keep items that could be gnawed out of a young puppy's reach and make sure

you provide a wide range of chews around the home to distract your pet from resorting to the furniture.

As your dog grows older, he will become bigger and more confident. He may start jumping up onto chairs to steal food left on a table—some dogs are even tall enough, when standing on their hind legs, to reach up and take food directly off a work surface or table. This is normal behavior rather than an indication that your pet is hungry, because dogs will instinctively take food at almost any opportunity—they are scavengers by nature, like wolves. Remember to keep food out of their reach at all times, especially when you are preparing a meal. It

Markings may vary quite widely, even in the case of purebred dogs such as dalmatians.

Dognosis
Sign Language

You will know by his body language if your dog understands that he has behaved poorly; he will keep his tail low, and if his ears are normally erect, they will droop down alongside his head as he adopts a submissive posture.

may be safer to shut your dog in another part of the home while you are cooking so he will not have the opportunity to steal any food. Do not leave shopping bags containing food on the floor when you come in, because this is placing temptation directly in your pet's path.

If your dog does manage to steal food, there is probably little you can do other than to scold him, especially if most of it has been eaten. If you need to take food away from your dog, do not approach him. Instead, close the door to the room so that your pet cannot run off, then capture his attention, telling him in a stern

voice to sit if he is standing over the food. Open his mouth and either remove the food directly or allow it to drop out onto the floor so you can pick it up. Finally, ignore your dog and walk off with the food. Certain foods that are favorites of ours—notably chocolate—are poisonous to dogs, so you need to be absolutely certain that these are kept out of your pet's reach at all times.

Temperature Shifts

Puppies tend to sleep longer than adult dogs. They often start by curling up in a ball, then shift position and stretch out. This is the way they control their body temperature: Curling up traps warm air close to their bodies, but once a puppy is warm and comfortable, he stretches out onto his side. Some breeds feel the cold more than others, either because they have relatively little hair on their bodies—the Mexican hairless, for example—or they lack a thick insulation undercoat, like the whippet. Puppies are especially vulnerable to the cold because they have a large surface area in relation to their volume, so heat escapes more rapidly than in an adult of the same breed. Provide a snug coat for your puppy to wear out in the backyard or when going for a walk in cold weather. A lightweight summer coat to keep off the rain is also a good idea because puppies do not like getting wet since their coats provide little protection against the elements.

Dognosis
Mealtimes

When introducing two dogs, irrespective of their ages, you need to be careful at feeding time because one dog may try to steal the other's food. Always feed them separately to avoid any risk of conflict. Puppies will require more meals than an adult dog.

Puppies are usually much more adaptable than older dogs in terms of settling into a household. A puppy may form a strong bond with a dog that is already established in the home.

Puppies grow up in a structured pack environment, learning from older dogs around them. In the home a young dog will soon come to regard itself as part of your pack and will therefore look to you for leadership. This simplifies the process of training.

Multipet Household

If you have other pets, your puppy will need to form a bond with them. Introducing a puppy to an older dog is relatively simple because the puppy is likely to defer to the older one, especially at first, significantly reducing the risk of conflict. Even though your instinct will be to make a greater fuss of your new puppy, helping him to settle in, it is most important that you do not undermine the standing of your established pet in the hierarchy. Praise him more than before, always giving him attention ahead of the puppy and being careful not to exclude him.

Older Dogs

Introducing two older dogs may be more difficult. If you bring the new dog home without warning, they are more likely to disagree because your established pet will instinctively be territorial and resent the intrusion of a stranger into his home environment. Allow them to meet first, preferably several times on neutral territory—on

Two's Company

There can be advantages to acquiring a second dog, although keep in mind the effect this will have on your budget. Introducing a puppy often gives a new lease on life to an older dog. From a more selfish standpoint, it may be less traumatic for you when your older dog ultimately passes away, because you will still have a dog in your life that will rely on you to look after him.

a walk, for instance, where they can run and play together and get to know each other. Once again, take care not to undermine your existing pet's status as "top dog."

Be observant so you can prevent potential disputes before they erupt. Although two dogs will generally agree, each is likely to display their own individual quirks—perhaps being possessive toward a favored toy. Some breeds are likely to get along better than others, depending on their origins. Those that were used for dogfighting in the past, such as the Staffordshire bull terrier, are less likely to tolerate a companion— especially one of their own kind— than a beagle, for example, which was traditionally kept in packs. There is no great worry about size, though, since large dogs can live with small ones— and in some cases the smaller dog may prove to be feistier.

Dogs and Cats

If you bring a young puppy into a home with a cat, you will need to supervise them carefully. Initially, your puppy will probably want to play with your cat, but a cat will be far less inclined to respond. It is more likely to hiss and snarl instead and may even lash out with its claws. Be especially careful with breeds such as the pug, because their prominent eyes are vulnerable to injury and their sight could be permanently impaired.

The puppy will soon lose interest in the cat when his continued attempts to play are rebuffed, though he is likely to persist in trying to steal the cat's food. Over time the two pets may strike up a bond and even curl up to sleep together, sharing a bed or the sofa. This is likely if you obtain a kitten and puppy at roughly

This puppy is simply being curious about the kitten, but if he does not heed the young cat's warning, he is likely to end up being scratched. Supervise encounters at first when introducing a dog to your home.

the same time so they grow up together. Introducing a kitten to an older dog can be more of a problem because the kitten will not be so assertive and is likely to be bullied by the dog unless you supervise them closely. However, cats will generally jump out of harm's way if threatened.

Rescued greyhounds, which are usually very gentle dogs, are unlikely to agree well with cats; this can be dangerous because a greyhound possesses the speed to outrun a cat and could kill her. The risk is not within the home but out in the backyard, where the greyhound may instinctively chase the cat, regarding her in a similar way to a hare. It may be a good idea to keep your pet muzzled if he displays any desire to chase after cats.

Dogs and Other Small Pets

Some household pets—notably rabbits, but also other small animals—are the natural quarry of dogs, so it is very important to keep them separate. Despite occasional stories in the news about a puppy forming a close bond with a young rabbit, for example, the risk that a dog may revert to its predatory instincts is always present. Small pets such as rabbits are also likely to be stressed by the presence of a dog nearby, even if the dog is just being curious.

Birds can react in the same way, becoming very anxious, and should not be let out of their cages while your dog is in the room.

If you let your rabbit out on the lawn in a run, do not leave your dog in the backyard unsupervised at the same time, because he may try to gain access to the run, either by trying to dig under the wire or by climbing on top. This is likely to be accompanied by excited barking, especially with a young dog. A similar response is likely if you have a tortoise wandering around the garden, because these reptiles are often a great source of fascination to puppies. The initial nervousness should pass in due course, but you need to be certain that your dog will not switch to picking up the tortoise and walking around with it as if it were a toy!

Dogs rarely show any interest in fish, but they may sometimes wade into a pond, especially a retriever or a dog of similar ancestry, which has a natural affiliation to water.

Be very wary about letting an adult dog off the leash for the first time. You must first take the time to build a strong bond between you and become confident that your pet will respond readily to your instructions.

Training

Dogs generally have a friendly disposition, especially toward members of the immediate family whom they know well. With a puppy it helps if all members of the family are involved in his care so your pet does not become more responsive to one person than another—which can lead to problems in the future, particularly with more assertive breeds, such as the rottweiler. If your pet becomes a one-person dog, he will be less inclined to respond to other people in the household and may even be hostile toward them.

Your tone of voice is a very important tool when communicating with your dog. Always speak in an enthusiastic tone when calling or praising him. Harsh tones should be reserved strictly for when you are displeased with him. Puppies do come to understand the meaning of words—with regard to sound—but as with all aspects of training, it is vital to be consistent because you can easily confuse your puppy. This should be practiced right from the outset.

Teaching Basic Commands
When you call your puppy to eat, always say, "Sit," before putting down the food bowl. If your pet fails to respond at first, do not tease him with the food. Instead, gently place a

A Dog's Tale
The Big Outdoors
Most puppies are acquired before they have completed their course of immunizations, so it is not safe to take them out. The only trip that should be undertaken at this stage is to your local veterinarian, when the puppy is about three months old. As well as handling the immunization, your vet will be able to check on the overall health of the young dog and advise on health-care issues, such as deworming. Even at the vet's office, try to keep your new pet away from other dogs to guard against the risk of acquiring any infection during the visit.

This puppy is asking to play. His characteristic posture is described as a play bow, and if you react by throwing a toy for him, he will spring up and chase after it.

hand over his hindquarters to encourage him to sit. This is a natural posture for dogs—especially if they are observing or waiting—so a young puppy will almost instinctively start reacting as required, associating the sound "sit" with the posture required.

Reinforce this message by getting your pet to sit at other times during the day, and before long your pet will have mastered this basic instruction. It is very important to ensure that your dog will sit readily when commanded. Although a small puppy jumping up may not be a source of worry, if an Irish wolfhound or similar large breed behaves in this way, it can be very disconcerting. It can even be dangerous under certain circumstances, since it may result in a child or older person being inadvertently knocked over.

You may also want to teach your puppy to lie down from a sitting position, which again is a natural shift. To show your puppy what is required, gently lower his front legs, saying, "Down," at the same time. Ask him to adopt this posture after a period of exercise, when he is tired, because this is the way that dogs rest after a run and before they curl up and go to sleep.

Wearing a Collar

The early time spent at home is a vital stage in your puppy's development, when you can start teaching key lessons that you can build upon once you can go out for

Introduce the collar by leaving it on your puppy for a couple of hours at a time. He is likely to try to remove it at first but will soon become accustomed to it.

walks together. The first step is to acquire a suitable collar for your puppy; there are various designs on the market, but at this stage a soft collar is recommended. It is important to check that the collar fits snugly, but at the same time it must not be too tight, because the puppy will be growing. It will need adjusting as your puppy's neck becomes bigger—check regularly to ensure that it is always loose enough to slide two fingers underneath. Attach an identity tag to the collar, engraved with a phone number—this will make it

Microchipping

Losing a pet can be heartbreaking. Recently, pet owners have turned to microchipping, a process whereby a tiny microchip is inserted just under the flap of skin in between a dog's shoulder blades. Most veterinarians and shelters have scanners that can read the chip, revealing its number. They then call the microchip company, who has the chip's number in their database and can provide the pet's information so that owner and dog can be reunited.

Many dogs are very athletic and are able to leap up off the ground to catch a ball. However, they can be just as adept at leaping over barriers, so you must ensure that your backyard is well fenced.

Dognosis Hand Signals

Dogs not only respond to verbal commands but also visual cues, just as members of a wolf pack communicate silently when hunting. Use your hands to reinforce training instructions, such as keeping your hand with palm outstretched as a sign that you want your dog to sit, and lowering your hand to show you want your dog to lie down. If you teach these signs to your puppy at an early stage, it will make things much easier once you start taking him out for walks.

much easier for someone finding your dog to contact you if he decides to stray, although he should also be microchipped for identity purposes (see box on page 71).

At first your puppy may be upset about wearing a collar, often rolling around on the ground and trying to reach it with his mouth or push it off with his legs. This phase will soon pass, after which you can attach a leash to the collar and start teaching your dog to walk alongside you. This will demand patience on your part,

because he probably will resent being restrained. Be prepared for your puppy to roll around again or pull on the leash. This behavior emphasizes the need to begin training early; although it is not difficult to restrain a young dog weighing only

10 lb (4.5 kg), an adult dog, which could be ten times heavier, is capable of dragging you both into danger.

On the Leash
Even though your puppy may be difficult to control on the leash at first, it is important to speak encouragingly to him and to use a positive tone. A puppy needs to be shown by example what is required, so it helps if you have a wall or fence in your backyard that can be used in the training sessions. You want your puppy to walk along beside you on your left in accordance with your pace, neither pulling ahead nor lagging behind. To prevent him from pulling away from you, try walking alongside a wall—effectively sandwiching the puppy between you and this barrier.

Always keep training sessions short, lasting no more than about 10 minutes or so, because dogs have a limited attention span. Always praise your pet when he reacts as required; do not scold him if he fails to respond correctly, because this can result in confusion and uncertainty in his mind. You will need to be patient and remember that a young dog may respond better one day than the next—this does not mean that lessons previously learned have

been forgotten. There could be something distracting or upsetting your dog that you are unaware of, such as a cat climbing around in a tree or an approaching thunderstorm. Do not worry about this; it is quite normal. Training is simply a matter of perseverance and positive reinforcement. In this case the better alternative would be to terminate the session early.

Carry on going through the basics with your dog, ideally carrying out at least three or four brief training sessions every day, and you should soon see an improvement. Once he is showing evident signs of progress and responding well, start to introduce additional aspects of training. One of the most important will be to link "sit" into the walking routine—this will be essential when you are out and need to stop to cross a road, for example.

Treats and Training
Although praise and the tone of your voice is important, many owners choose to reward good behavior with treats. These should be used

A leash for a puppy needs to be durable, although you should try to keep it out of your puppy's reach so he cannot chew it.

73

sparingly; otherwise, your dog will become fixated on receiving a treat and will look for this rather than concentrating on what he should be doing.

Using treats each time that a dog responds well is also creating problems for the future, because this type of food can have a seriously detrimental effect on your pet's health.

Commercial treats are full of calories, so using them regularly means your dog will be at risk of obesity, which can lead to health problems such as diabetes mellitus.

If you decide to use treats, opt for healthy items, such as a piece of carrot or a slice of apple—but even in this case, do not give a treat every time your dog responds as required. Rationing treats will help to improve your dog's level of concentration because he will be focusing on what you are asking rather than looking for an inevitable reward. Offering a treat at the end of the session is a better idea, indicating that it has finished, although there is actually no need to use any treats as part of the training process. Puppies can be trained just as effectively using positive reinforcement only.

Dognosis
Open Wide

Training your puppy to allow you to open his mouth will make it much easier when you need to brush his teeth or give him medication. Older dogs that have not had their mouths opened in this way from an early age can be very difficult to handle and may bite you, not because they are aggressive but because they are fearful. If you need to give a tablet, you will have to stand behind your pet to stop him from backing away and hold his head while someone else tries to administer it. Another alternative is to disguise it in his food.

Do not worry if your puppy yawns and sleeps during the day. This is normal behavior. Puppies tend to have brief periods of intense activity and then fall asleep quite suddenly.

The Importance of Routine

Dogs are very much creatures of habit, so a puppy will fit into your lifestyle more easily than an older dog, who will have grown up in different surroundings. Maintaining a routine is part of the training process, because if your dog is allowed out regularly at set times, the likelihood of accidents within the home is reduced. Dogs also develop an innate instinct for when a meal is due, so be sure to stick to the set times closely or your dog will become restless and distressed.

Traveling Together

Even before it is safe to take your puppy out in public, it is a good idea to take him for a drive in a car so he becomes familiar with this experience and learns how to behave. Do not worry if he is sick initially—motion sickness caused by the unfamiliar sensations of moving in this way usually passes as your pet becomes used to being in the car.

You must ensure that your puppy learns to travel safely. Do not allow any dog, especially a puppy, to travel unrestrained in a vehicle. If your pet distracts you momentarily when you are driving, you could end up in a serious, if not fatal, crash. Young puppies are best confined in special traveling crates, lined in newspaper with a cushion on top. This is also the best way for toy breeds to travel. Larger dogs should either be behind a grille across the back of the car or have a harness—resembling a seatbelt—with a seat cover to sit on. Your dog will need to be accustomed to this, but make sure that you stay in the vehicle throughout this process so that he will not scratch at the seat covering, trying to break free.

A major reason for taking a puppy out on trips is that dogs can otherwise come to associate being taken out in a car with going out for a walk and become very excited, misbehaving and often barking persistently. It can be disconcerting if you need to go on a long drive with your dog and he persists in howling all the way. Short trips out, which do not necessarily result in a walk, will help to avoid this problem from arising in the future.

A Cautionary Note

The temperature within a vehicle can rise rapidly within minutes on a hot summer day, especially if it is parked in direct sunlight. Never leave your dog alone under such circumstances. Even leaving a window partly open will not be enough to protect your pet from the effects of heat stroke, which are likely to prove fatal. It is better to leave your dog at home than run the risk, but if you must take him, park only where the vehicle will not be exposed to sunlight in an underground parking lot.

Do not exclude your dog from a game, because he may become resentful and start barking loudly, displaying his frustration. Also, in a public place such as a park, he may run off and seize a ball elsewhere, which could cause serious problems.

The Significance of Play

Playtime is one of the best ways to bond with your puppy. There are many toys produced specially for dogs, but it is not essential to buy a large number. In most cases a chew toy and a ball, which your dog can run after and retrieve, should be sufficient.

Puppies are excited by play and are eager to do so any chance they can. Like children, it helps them to learn skills and develops their coordination. Some breeds—such as retrievers—may be more enthusiastic about chasing after a ball than others, but most dogs will soon learn to play and bring it back to you. Be careful when throwing the toy, because some

rubber toys can be quite heavy and therefore painful if they hit your pet.

Always call your pet by name to encourage him to return to you with the toy, reinforcing the message for when you call him to you at other times. Puppies soon learn that coming back means there is likely to be another opportunity for a game. When your dog returns with the toy in his mouth, encourage him to drop it, reinforced by the instruction "Drop." At first your puppy may not obey, and if he runs off when you try to grasp the toy, do not chase after him; he will consider this to be part of the game. Stand your ground, and once he is within reach again, gently grasp his collar to restrain him.

To take the toy out of his jaws, hold the lower jaw firmly along the sides with your right hand (if you are right-handed), then place your left hand on either side of the upper jaw, lifting it up so the mouth opens and the toy falls to the ground. Pick up the toy and throw it again immediately— before long your puppy will learn that if the game is to continue, the toy must be dropped.

This is a very important lesson to teach from the outset, because puppies often pick up objects they should not. Shoes of any kind are often a favorite, as well as mobile phones and remote-control units for electrical equipment. If you are able to persuade your dog to release such items on command, it may save them from being irreparably damaged.

Rescued Dogs

You need to be sensitive if acquiring an adult dog from a rescue center. If the dog has been mistreated, he can be exceptionally nervous and may have bad memories, which can surface suddenly and unexpectedly. Even simply putting on a jacket of a particular color might upset your dog, recalling a painful incident from his past. It is really important to try to discover as much as possible about the history of a rescue dog at the outset, although this can be much more difficult than it sounds. Some dogs may have gone through a series of homes, or they may have been simply abandoned on the street, which means there are no resources to rely upon for any past history.

Responsible rescue organizations always try to build up a detailed profile of any dog that comes into their care so that they can try to match him to a new home. However, while it is possible to gauge whether a dog is scared of men, for example, there will be many other behavioral traits that may become apparent only in the domestic

environment. Should you encounter problems, such as separation anxiety—which is a common problem in rescue dogs—then your vet or the rescue center itself should be able to refer you to an experienced behaviorist to help the dog overcome such problems.

Dogs from shelters are usually not well trained, but until you get to know your new pet at home, you will not be able to assess his behavior. It is harder to train an adult dog than a puppy, and you will need to be tolerant up to a point. On the other hand, you can sign an older dog up for training

Remember that young dogs do not have the foresight to detect potential danger that comes with age and experience, especially in new environments.

classes right away and start working to correct his behavioral problems. Dog-training classes are often advertised in local newspapers, or you can ask your veterinarian for advice. Much depends on your dog's particular requirements—the behaviorist will be able to carry out an accurate assessment for you.

Out and About

Taking your dog out for a walk helps to keep him fit by providing exercise, but it also keeps him mentally alert. This is clear from the way that a young dog sleeps after taking a walk, even though he may not have covered much distance. Your dog will be able to go out in public at about four months old, which provides a good opportunity to let him experience a wide range of situations. This will help to overcome any instinctive fears that he may have, making it easier to travel with him in the future. Remember that to a puppy everything will be strange at first because he will not have been outside the confines of your home and backyard—except possibly in a car. You need to progress slowly; just taking your dog down the road will open up his world significantly. He will not only be seeing and hearing different things, just as we would, but also detecting a wide range of new scents. Even if your puppy is trained to walk on the leash at home, his behavior is likely to lapse when he first starts going out, because there will be so many distractions.

Dognosis Back to School

Young dogs can go to socialization classes, where they learn how to interact in a friendly and controlled way with other dogs. This is very important with certain types of dog; sight hounds, such as greyhounds, for example, can be rather shy—especially with strangers—but meeting people at a young age can help overcome this trait. Breeds that tend not to be friendly toward other dogs, such as Staffordshire bull terriers, will also benefit from such classes; they will learn to accept fellow dogs at an early stage, reducing the risk that they will be hostile toward them later in life.

The Learning Experience

When they are first taken out, young dogs may be frightened by vehicles going past or by the presence of other pedestrians on the sidewalk. Your pet may pause frequently—perhaps looking around with his tail tucked down between his legs and his ears held down, which indicates his uncertain state of mind. Provide him with plenty of reassurance; let him pause and see what is going on around him. This will help to reassure him, but also speak to him softly, using his name, to let him know that there is nothing to worry about. Do not take

him very far on these early excursions. Instead, allow him to experience a range of different situations. You will notice his confidence begin to increase. He will look forward to going out, and he will run out to see you if he hears you putting on your coat. Start to build a ritual so your puppy does not develop bad habits. Make sure that he sits down so you can put his leash on easily, rather than leaping about with excitement at the thought of going out, which will make it very difficult.

When you begin taking your puppy out to a park, where he is likely to meet other dogs for the first time,

do not let him off the leash until you are fairly certain that he will return to you when called. This is something that you will need to practice at home. Have another member of the family hold the puppy, then head off some distance away and call your dog to you using his name—once he is released, he should run toward you. Give him plenty of praise and then get him to sit. After a run is when you will need to attach the leash to his collar.

Letting Go
Letting your puppy off the leash for the first time can be worrisome. You need to be certain that he has

The younger dog on the right is slightly wary and watching what his older companion is doing. In time your pet will become more confident.

mastered the basics of training, coming back to you when called and staying readily when told to do so. This is vital to keep him away from any potential dangers that you may encounter unexpectedly while out for a walk. As an interim step, take him out on an extendible leash so when you are in relatively open countryside, you can let the leash out and your dog can wander farther away from you. At this point reinforce the training message by calling him back at intervals and he will soon learn that he needs to come back to you when called. You can reward him occasionally with a healthy treat, such as a piece of carrot, but do not give him something to eat on every occasion.

On the first few occasions, carefully choose the area in which to let him off the leash. You do not want your puppy to become so excited that he simply bounds away into the distance, forgetting you are around. Rather than letting your dog run free as soon as you get out of your vehicle, it is better to walk with him for some distance. This will mean that

Dogs and Farm Animals

It is important not to let your dog off the leash where you are likely to encounter farm stock. Many dogs are instinctively curious about sheep, for example, and will go bounding up to them, which can cause mass panic and be disastrous in a field of pregnant ewes. Even if the adult sheep are not actually attacked, their fear can result in loss of unborn lambs. On the other hand, a young dog venturing into a field of cattle may be trampled or kicked severely.

he is less excitable and will be more inclined to stay with you rather than running off ahead. This is especially important if you have chosen somewhere you do not walk regularly with your dog, because it will be unfamiliar to him.

Reinforcing the Bond

Your dog will encounter new experiences when you are out for a walk, so you need to reinforce the bond between you in this new environment. Call him back regularly throughout the walk to get him into the habit of returning readily. Choose an open area of countryside, partly so you and your dog can see each other when you let him run free. This also provides an opportunity for you to play with your dog, which will again reinforce your bond and discourage him from roaming off on his own. Take a ball along to throw for him to chase, encouraging him to bring it back to you as he would at home. Dogs learn very quickly, and your pet will be less likely to disappear into the distance.

Keeping in Touch

There may be times when your pet does stray far from you. If this happens, a high-frequency dog whistle—which is inaudible to our ears—can be useful, but start by using it when your pet is nearby so that he becomes accustomed to the sound: Give a couple of blasts on the whistle, then call your pet back to you. Before long he will associate the sound of the whistle with coming back to you—and may also use it to track your position and find his way back when you are out of sight. In open country, hand signals can be useful to communicate with your pet from some distance away. You can beckon him back by arm movements or instruct him to stay by raising your hand upright, with the palm outstretched.

What to Do If Your Dog Disappears

A young dog is likely to be a little nervous when off the leash for the first few times and will not stray far, but as he becomes more confident, he will start exploring on his own—especially if you walk the same route regularly. Instincts take over with

some dogs, and they will set off to follow a scent. Don't attempt to run after him, because you are unlikely to catch up and, perceiving you as a fellow pack member, your dog is likely to be encouraged to run faster rather than to stop. The best thing is to stand your ground and call your dog back—after his initial burst of enthusiasm for the chase, he should return in due course. Do not scold him when he returns, even if you are feeling angry about him running off, because it will confuse him and weaken the bond between you.

If after about 15 minutes your dog still has not returned, set off in the same direction in case he is looking for you. Whistle regularly so he can locate you even if he cannot see you. The sound of a high-frequency dog whistle carries over a much wider area than an ordinary whistle. If you cannot find him, notify the police, veterinarians, and animal welfare organizations in the area in case he has been seen or picked up. This is where microchipping is invaluable (see page 71); it will still be possible to reunite you with your pet even if your dog has lost his tag as a result of his exploits.

An older male dog is more likely to run off in a public park than

Taking part in agility competitions, such as racing against the clock around an obstacle course, is a great way to bond with your dog.

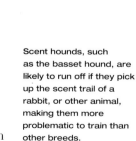

Scent hounds, such as the basset hound, are likely to run off if they pick up the scent trail of a rabbit, or other animal, making them more problematic to train than other breeds.

out in the countryside, because the scent of any nearby bitch on heat will attract him. She will be producing special scent molecules called pheromones, which are wafted on the air over considerable distances and will be detected by every male dog in the neighborhood. If a dog has been neutered, he will not respond, helping to curb any instinctive desire to wander in pursuit.

Keeping Watch

When you take your dog to a new area, beware of any potential risks. Many dogs love going to a beach, but make sure your pet does not pick up pebbles that he might either swallow or chew, which could damage his teeth. Currents can be another hazard if your dog decides to swim. Do not encourage him to climb on breakwaters, because he might slip into the sea, and watch for broken pieces of glass, sharp metal cans, or other debris that could lacerate your dog's paws if he walks over them. Remember to take a drinking container and a bottle of water for your pet if you are intending to spend any time on the beach, because he might be tempted to drink the seawater, which may in turn make him ill.

Be responsible and keep your dog on a leash in areas where there are other people around—especially children playing with balls or picnicking, because your dog may frighten them by trying to join in.

Park Life

When out walking in a park, there can be a number of distractions for your pet: ball games, kites, people jogging or Roller-blading. Your dog needs to become accustomed to seeing all of these, quite apart from meeting other dogs, so start by taking him out during the early morning, when the park is likely to be quiet. You will probably be able to let him off for a good run at this time and then give him another walk on the leash in the late afternoon or early evening, when there are likely to be more people around. Allow him time to watch what is going on so that he can learn and will not be frightened as he walks with you. This is important to ensure that your puppy grows up into a well-balanced adult dog.

Dog's Tale
Dogs that Wander

Certain types of dog are more likely to run off than others: Scent hounds, such as the beagle or basset hound, are most likely to stray, while a toy breed is less likely to wander. However, do not assume that a small dog is less likely to vanish than a larger one, because terriers, for instance, are certainly inclined to go off exploring. Their size and instincts mean they may venture down foxholes or rabbit warrens, vanishing underground. Keep a wary eye on your dog at all times or you may turn around to find that he has disappeared unexpectedly from sight—and a young dog is quite likely to become trapped. Sight hounds may also race off, but in most cases they do not display the stamina of scent hounds, so they are less likely to vanish into the distance.

Meeting Strangers

Some people, especially children, do not know how to approach dogs without frightening them. Be alert when there are children near your dog, because they may try to stroke him without warning—and your dog may misinterpret the sudden movement as an aggressive lunge toward you. He may react by snapping at them, which is obviously not to be encouraged. If your pet is used to meeting other people outside your family circle regularly, however, he will be less perturbed by an unfamiliar greeting.

Talk with Your Dog

Dogs communicate very much like people, using

a combination of vocalizations and body language.

This allows us to gain insight into their moods and

behavior and not only understand what they are saying

but also develop a dialogue. And in some ways their

ability to sense and communicate facts about their surroundings

exceeds our own, proving they are very valuable companions, able to

detect problems and warn us when we are in danger.

Barking, Growling, and Whimpering

The sound most commonly associated with dogs is barking. Dogs bark for various reasons, sometimes simply because they are excited or sometimes as a warning. It is not always easy to distinguish between the different sounds of a dog's bark, because much depends on the circumstances. A dog who knows you well is likely to bark as a greeting when he sees you. But if you meet a strange dog in unfamiliar surroundings, its bark is likely to have a deeper pitch and a more menacing tone because it is intended more as a warning than a greeting. The actual sound of a dog's bark differs slightly, depending not only on the breed but also the particular dog, so you will be able to recognize your dog's bark even if he is out of view.

The Reasons Behind the Bark
Barking is not just a warning gesture; dogs will also bark for other reasons. One type signifies excitement, and it often happens when you come home,

A Dog's Tale
Barks and Breeds

Some dogs instinctively bark more than others, and guard dogs, such as rottweilers, possess a deep threatening bark. Many small dogs can also be noisy—the sound of their bark bears no relation to their stature and often suggests a much larger animal. This is because many small companion breeds were bred to watch over their aristocratic owners, alerting them to potential danger at close quarters. Pugs have a particular reputation for loyalty—Josephine's pet pug bit the French emperor Napoleon on their wedding night. Earlier in history another pug saved the life of Prince William of Orange by alerting him to the presence of a would-be assassin.

Dogs will bark for a variety of reasons, although usually out of excitement or as a warning.

if your pet is waiting to be taken out for a walk or if he wants to play a game. In this case the barks are short and repeated as part of a sequence, becoming louder and taking on a more urgent tone if your dog feels that he is being ignored.

Your dog may also bark if he needs your assistance—perhaps he is shut out in the backyard and cannot get back in. Do not encourage this behavior, because it can cause a disturbance, especially if you allow your dog to stay outside for long periods or late at night. The solution is to take the initiative from puppyhood, calling your dog back in after he has been out for a set period of time so he does not become conditioned to bark for your attention. However, you may still occasionally find that your dog barks to be let out of a room, particularly if he feels that he is being ignored.

Dogs may also bark if they are uncertain—this behavior is often common in a young dog out for a walk. The sound is usually a staccato series of barks with a tone of greater urgency, unlike repeated barking to attract your attention. This barking requires urgent investigation because it might indicate that your dog is in danger. Call your dog back to you immediately and try to locate him right away if he fails to respond and simply continues barking.

Age also has an impact on how often a dog will bark, because young dogs are instinctively more vocal than

Dognosis Noisy by Nature

Some dogs are known to be noisier while some are quieter than others, and over the years this aspect of their natural behavior has been encouraged, depending on the breed. Many sight hounds—such as greyhounds, which were bred originally for hunting—are quiet by nature compared with other breeds, because owners did not want their dogs attracting attention when they were out hunting. A noisy dog would lose the element of surprise. For instance, lurchers, which are a cross between a greyhound and a collie, are favored because they work in complete silence. In contrast, terriers have found a role as good farm watchdogs, because they bark to alert their owners when strangers arrive.

older ones. This is partly a reflection of their more excitable nature, and also due to their lack of experience, which means that they are less certain about the world in general. Barking is also how a puppy learns to keep in close touch with his mother and littermates.

Changing Tones

A dog's bark will change in tone according to the situation. Your dog may bark when you arrive home, but the sound of his voice will be very different in both intensity and frequency if a stranger comes to the door. The bark for you is a greeting, but for a stranger it is a sign of aggression, intended to intimidate. It will become louder and more threatening if it is not heeded.

Dogs also sometimes bark to attract attention to themselves,

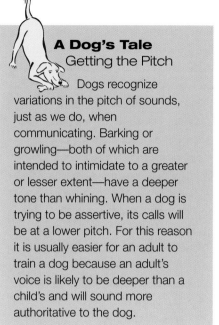

A Dog's Tale
Getting the Pitch

Dogs recognize variations in the pitch of sounds, just as we do, when communicating. Barking or growling—both of which are intended to intimidate to a greater or lesser extent—have a deeper tone than whining. When a dog is trying to be assertive, its calls will be at a lower pitch. For this reason it is usually easier for an adult to train a dog because an adult's voice is likely to be deeper than a child's and will sound more authoritative to the dog.

especially if they are left alone for long periods each day, which can be annoying for other people in the vicinity and lead to complaints from neighbors. This type of barking indicates separation anxiety (see pages 174–75): Your dog is feeling disorientated and abandoned. Nervous animals are prone to behave this way, especially those dogs who have been rescued from a bad home, because they feel abandoned again when left alone and they are seeking reassurance.

Old dogs may bark persistently at night if they become seriously disoriented when left alone in the dark. This is usually a symptom of canine cognitive dysfunction (CCD), a medical condition that has similarities to human Alzheimer's disease and calls for veterinary help.

You will soon be able to recognize your own dog by the sound of his bark. As dogs get older, the intensity of their bark tends to decrease.

Growling with Intent

At close quarters dogs use a variety of other calls of differing intensity to indicate their mood—the most common is growling. As with barking, growling often serves as an aggressive warning, but it can also be an indication of playfulness, so it needs to be interpreted in accordance with the dog's body language (see page 92) and the pitch of the sound.

When a dog is growling as a warning, the sound will become louder and more menacing, and it will be combined with aggressive body language such as raised hackles. The dog's overall intention is to intimidate his opponent into backing down without the need for a fight.

Sometimes—especially in the case of young dogs playing together—growling is simply a way of expressing friendly rivalry, so it lacks the intensity that could lead to serious conflict. Your dog may also utter this sound during a game, particularly when playing with a tug toy. It is not usually aggressive in this context; it's just a friendly means of trying to inhibit you—like two young dogs playing with each other.

If you are out together and your dog starts growling, it probably indicates that he has spotted something nearby that he is uncertain about; he may have chosen not to bark, because the danger is close at hand. There will be other signs of uncertainty in his body language: He will freeze in position, looking directly toward what has disturbed him, often with his hackles raised as another sign of nervousness. You are more likely to see these signs in young dogs, who are still learning about the world around them. The object of

If a dog barks continuously and rapidly, this usually indicates that he has encountered something nearby that is worrying him.

concern may be something such as a plastic bag hooked in the grass and inflated by the wind. However, depending on where you live, it could also be a venomous snake in the grass, so be careful when you investigate.

Whining

Whining is another call that has specific meaning. Dogs whine in order to attract attention and to indicate frustration. They do so in a variety of situations, and the sound will become increasingly loud and frequent, escalating into barking if ignored. In the home your dog may whine because he wants your help—perhaps to let him in or out of a door.

Whining is also common if something your dog is expecting has not materialized—for example, if

you arrive home after his usual mealtime and he is waiting to be fed, or you are late to take him out for a walk. The sound will become more intense when you stand up, because your dog will know that this is a sign that you are likely to feed him or look for his leash.

Whimpering

Whimpering is a less intense version of whining, and it is one of the most direct ways that dogs communicate with their owners at close quarters. Whimpering demands a response because it may signify that there is something wrong, and especially with small dogs, this can create a problem. Your dog will soon learn that making these calls immediately attracts your attention, so he will start to whimper

Size is not everything—some toy breeds can make formidable guardians. A pet pug once saved a Dutch prince by barking loudly when a would-be assassin broke into the royal quarters.

or whine whenever he wants you to respond. For this reason it is very important to learn to distinguish between whimpering for a reason, when your dog genuinely requires your assistance, and situations where he is just seeking attention. If you don't, you can rapidly find yourself becoming controlled by your pet!

Whimpering Outdoors

Whimpering heard outdoors takes on a more serious dimension because it is usually an indication of pain. If your dog hurts himself—perhaps cutting his foot by stepping on a piece of glass or an old nail—he will pull up short and start whimpering loudly. You can easily spot the problem, because your dog will be reluctant to place weight on the affected leg and he will be holding it off the ground, even if he tries to walk a few steps. Take care when trying to examine the wound, because it will be painful and your dog may snap at you with very little warning.

If your dog is involved in a fight and his opponent chases him off, he may run away whimpering. This is not necessarily an indication that he is in pain because of a physical injury—it is simply a vocal means of reinforcing his submissive body language toward the other dog. Even so, once your dog returns to you, be sure to check that he has not been injured.

As dogs become older, they tend to put on weight, so they are more likely to start snoring regularly.

Dognosis
Grunting, Snoring, and Sleeping

When your dog is relaxed and apparently asleep, he might make grunts that sound similar to very loud hiccups—these are usually signs of contentment. Dogs also snore, just as people do, with the same contributory factors. Older, overweight pets are most at risk, as well as breeds with compact faces, such as bulldogs and pugs. Once your dog wakes up, he may yawn loudly and stretch, just as many people do when they get out of bed. When a dog stretches, he usually pushes his front legs out straight, extending and lowering the front part of his body before arching his back.

Body Language

A dog who is concerned about approaching strangers may display an aggressive tone to his bark, and his body language may seem aggressive as well. The position of his ears and tail are very important indicators of a dog's mood, even if he is not barking.

Reading the Ear Position

When a dog is lively and curious, his ears are drawn forward slightly from their normal resting position, and they are often lifted up slightly. If you reprimand your pet in a stern voice, however, his ears are likely to be held back low against the sides of his head, creating what is sometimes described as a "hangdog" look.

When you are out walking with your pet, you may find that he pauses with one ear raised and the other one lowered. This is very common—especially in young dogs—and it indicates that your dog is uncertain about how to react to something.

Raised ears indicate that a dog is listening intently. If one ear is raised and the other lowered, it may mean your dog is uncertain about something.

This borzoi is relaxed but at the same time alert. The position of the ears is very significant in determining a dog's mood.

Tail Talk

Another important indicator of your dog's mood is the position of his tail, and this may be visible at some distance. If your pet is barking but is some distance away from you, one way to determine whether he is very nervous or just excited is to check his tail position. When happy and relaxed, a dog will wag his tail enthusiastically from side to side as a greeting and to show his pleasure, and he will generally keep it upright. If he is slightly nervous—but not feeling intimidated—he will keep his tail up but will not wag it so markedly, keeping it relatively still but quivering at the tip. His ears will also be drawn forward. In a situation where he feels under threat, a dog will hold his tail out horizontally, advancing with caution. When you scold your dog, he will probably adopt a subservient posture, curling his tail down between his legs. This is also the posture that a losing dog will exhibit when fleeing from the victor after a fight.

Tailless or Short-tailed Dogs

In some breeds dogs may be born without tails—such as old English sheepdogs, which are still sometimes referred to by their former name of bobtail—although not all puppies in a litter will be tailless. Other breeds have very short tails. The Pembroke Welsh corgi, for example, has a very short tail in contrast to its Cardigan cousin. Dogs with no tails or with small stumps have difficulty

A Dog's Tale
Communication and Ears

Not all dogs are able to converse easily with ear movements—for instance, the long, heavy, pendulous ears of most spaniels mean that they are not able to use them very effectively to communicate. Other breeds, such as the bearded collie, have ears that are mostly hidden by hair. Surgical ear cropping, which is still permitted in a number of countries, also interferes with this type of canine communication. The surgery removes part of the cartilage in each ear, making it less flexible: The dog's appearance is permanently transformed—its ears are held erect rather than lying down over the sides of the head. Great Danes, rottweilers, and dobermans are among the most common breeds for this operation because it makes them look more fierce.

This "play bow" position is often seen in young dogs. It is a sign that your pet is in a playful mood.

communicating, both with their owners and with other dogs. This breakdown in communication ability is one reason that tail docking is no longer universally practiced, even for show dogs. Docking involves removing a portion of a puppy's tail at birth to protect this part of the body from injury and is mainly used on working dogs (see page 39).

Shivering

If your dog starts to shiver, do not automatically assume that he is cold, especially if he is indoors. This reaction can also be a sign of pent-up excitement—for example, you may notice it when you are preparing your pet's food or if you are delayed by a phone call just as you are both ready to go out for a walk. Ultimately, your dog is likely to start barking excitedly, as well as shivering, if he feels the process is taking too long.

Dognosis
Weather Forecast

The weather has also been known to affect a dog's mood. During periods of hot, sultry weather, dogs can become more short-tempered than usual, and they are more likely to react aggressively—particularly toward children. This may be because their sensitivity to air pressure helps them detect an approaching storm, while humidity can make dogs with long and relatively thick coats very uncomfortable.

Welsh corgis are more inclined to nip than other breeds because they were bred to work with cattle, snapping at their heels to control them. This is not a sign of aggression.

Meeting People

Your dog's behavior toward other people is very important. Always remember that not everyone likes dogs; some people are frightened of them. When you are out for a walk with your pet, do not let him go bounding off to greet people and jump up at them with exuberance. This could easily be misinterpreted as a sign of aggression. Even worse, your dog may decide to run and join in on a children's ball game in a public park, creating some mayhem.

Children need to be supervised closely with dogs, and they must be taught not to tease them. Dogs consider children as lower in the pack hierarchy than adults, so breeds such as the doberman, which have a dominant nature, are more likely to challenge them.

When you are out with your dog, try to watch for potential problems

Puppies and children usually get along well, but supervise them to be sure their play does not become too rambunctious.

that may occur. Even in more rural areas your pet should not be wandering out of sight—especially if there are farm animals nearby. Always call him back to you at regular intervals. If you are in the countryside with a scent hound, such as a beagle, this approach may not stop your pet from heading off into the distance whenever he picks up an interesting scent, but it can help combat this instinctive behavior.

It is important to keep in touch with your dog when you are out for a walk because this contact mimics the way in which members of a wolf pack communicate when they are on the move through their territory, and it will reinforce the bond between you and your pet.

Calling Him Back

Make it a habit to call back your dog when you are out on a walk together—he will learn to listen for your call or whistle and come back to you. That way, if you need to call him back quickly for a reason, he will react to you faster and in a relaxed way.

When Dog Meets Dog

Dogs tend to lead solitary lives now that they have been adopted into the human family rather than living in packs as their wild ancestors did. However, dogs who meet regularly—when out walking, for example—often establish a close bond. They will greet each other in a friendly way, wagging their tails and often barking excitedly at first, even after several months.

Dogs often sniff noses upon meeting, while staring intently at each other. Note the way in which the ears of both these dogs are drawn slightly back—a sign of uncertainty, with the dog on the right appearing more nervous.

Introducing Two Dogs

If you need to introduce two dogs, especially if they are ultimately going to share the same household, it is a good idea to let them meet on neutral territory. If possible, start by taking the two of them out for a long walk, allowing them to get to know each other in their own time without forcing them together. Once they have become acquainted, you may find them playing and chasing after each other—especially if they are young dogs. Initially, don't take a ball or a toy for them to chase, because one dog may become possessive, which will lead to a conflict. It is much better to allow the two dogs to run together—ultimately, they will cover more ground this way than if they were walked on a leash individually.

When they are tired, take the dogs home. But watch them carefully at first until they have settled down. As the leader of the pack, it is important for you to communicate how you expect them to behave together. Although your instinctive inclination may be to encourage the newcomer—who may be somewhat withdrawn and nervous in strange surroundings—it is vital to reinforce the position of the established pet. Do not expect your dog to give up his bed or his favorite place for the newcomer; this will simply be perceived as undermining your existing dog's position.

Mealtimes

Always remember that mealtimes are potential flash points, so be sure to feed each dog individually. Dogs instinctively gulp down their food just like wolves, without chewing it much, which allows them to grab as much as they can. If a dog tries to steal from his companion, it will almost certainly trigger an aggressive response.

Some dogs are more tolerant of their own breed than of others. So introducing a companion to a pack hound, such as a beagle, is likely to be easier than with a more territorial breed, such as a rottweiler. The dog's gender can also be significant: Intact male dogs are less tolerant than their neutered counterparts or bitches. Age can be another important factor. An older dog will be more inclined to accept a younger companion.

Dognosis In a Mood

Just like you, your dog may have moods. Bitches can be very determined to run away in search of a mate when they are in heat, while a male dog will try to escape if he detects the scent of a bitch nearby. There is a condition sometimes experienced by bitches known as false, or pseudo, pregnancy, so watch for behavioral changes that may indicate this. The signs will be apparent about eight weeks after her last period of heat—at a time when, if she had mated, she would be giving birth to puppies. She may develop a peculiar obsession with a certain toy, growling loudly and becoming aggressive if you try to take it away from her. This is the result of hormonal changes in her body that have led her to believe that she has been pregnant and cause her to see her toy as a surrogate puppy—in some cases, bitches even produce milk. This phase will pass, but the only long-term solution is to have her neutered.

Close Encounters

When two unfamiliar dogs meet off the leash, one is likely to go bounding up to the other. In some cases they will appear to like each other almost instantly, each sniffing the other's hindquarters. Their meeting may be

For centuries scent hounds have traditionally been kept in packs and, for this reason, tend to be more social than other breeds.

accompanied by vigorous tail wagging, although they may behave more cautiously. There is a greater risk of an aggressive response if one of the dogs is roaming free while the other is on a leash—the tethered animal will not be able to react normally, so it is more likely to respond aggressively.

Establishing Dominance

When dogs meet, there is usually a key moment when dominance is established. Both dogs will look each other straight in the eye at that first encounter, and the subservient dog will look away first. After this moment it is unlikely that there will be any serious dispute between the dogs. Even so, remember that some dogs are instinctively more combative by nature than others, which reflects their origins. Breeds such as bull terriers, which were once bred for

fighting purposes, are still more likely to assert themselves when confronted by another dog. This is especially common in mature male dogs that have not been neutered, because the higher levels of testosterone in their blood encourage aggressive behavior.

Dogfights

Dogs do not normally launch into fights without warning, because they are capable of inflicting serious injuries on each other. They tend to give off a series of warnings of increasing intensity, hoping to persuade a would-be rival to back down before the encounter escalates into a fight. At close quarters your dog will try to bluff his rival into backing down by trying to appear larger and more intimidating than usual. Dogs raise the area of fur known as their hackles—which runs along the back

Size Doesn't Matter

Do not assume that a large dog is less easily intimidated than its smaller rivals. Small dogs, especially those of terrier stock, can be very feisty and will not back away easily if they encounter a bigger rival. Terriers were often bred to pursue larger quarry. They would go underground to drive a fox out of its hiding spot, which required considerable bravery.

Play fighting serves a purpose: It allows young dogs to test their strength against each other without either being likely to get hurt.

Dognosis
Alpha Pairs

In wolf packs there is a recognizable hierarchy, which is necessary to maintain social cohesion within the group. The pack is headed by the alpha male and female, who form the dominant pair. A fight is likely to break out if a younger male decides to challenge the pack leader.

of the neck—when challenged. This serves as an obvious warning gesture, which is reinforced by your dog pulling back his lips to bare his teeth conspicuously. This behavior is likely to be accompanied by growling, which will become more intense if ignored.

Even at this stage, despite showing outward signs of aggressive behavior, neither dog is entirely confident. They will both be looking for the opportunity to escape from their rival if necessary. If a fight does break out, it will generally not last very long; the loser may be chased for a short distance by his opponent,

but rarely will the pursuer attack again. However, even a short burst of fighting can result in serious bite wounds—often to the ears, which tend to be fairly exposed as the dogs scuffle.

It can be dangerous to intervene directly by putting your hand down to pull your dog away if he is involved in a standoff. This sudden movement may be enough to encourage the dogs to start fighting. If you need to rescue your dog, use your leash as a lasso instead, dropping it down over his head from behind so you can drag him away from the potential conflict.

Touch
and Healing

Dogs generally love being stroked and
cuddled, and this will reinforce the
bond between you and your pet. It is very
important to begin handling a young
puppy early in life so he becomes
accustomed to it; otherwise, he will be nervous about being touched
later on. Stroking also provides the opportunity to make regular
health checks on your pet.

Stroking and Petting

Try to spend as much time as possible stroking your new puppy and engaging with him. He is small, so you can pick him up and stroke him, which has the additional advantage of reassuring him about being carried. Encourage all members of the family to make a fuss over the puppy so he grows accustomed to receiving attention from everyone—if not, your pet may become attached to one person in the household, making it harder for other family members to interact with him once he is older. Some breeds tend to be more one-person dogs than others, especially those that were bred primarily as guardians, such as the doberman pinscher. This is simply a sign of their natural protective instincts.

Stroking your dog is a tool you can use when training. For instance, you can use it as an acknowledgment that your dog is behaving the way you want. Puppies often wriggle around while you are trying to stroke them, but when they are tired, they will appreciate the opportunity to curl up alongside you and fall asleep while being stroked. This replicates the way a young dog curls up with his littermates and his mother when sleeping.

To stroke a puppy properly, start by placing your hand on top of the head and then running it backward down the length of the body. Dogs often like to have the area behind each ear stroked as well. When your dog is feeling very relaxed, he will roll over onto his back and allow you to stroke his chest and underparts. Encourage your dog to behave this way, because it can be useful if he will roll over onto his back to be groomed.

Children should be taught the importance of being gentle when it comes to handling and stroking a dog. They should also get into the habit of washing their hands after playing with their pet, certainly before eating.

Stroking for Health

As well as reinforcing the bond between you, stroking provides a great opportunity to keep a watch on your pet's health. While stroking, study his coat to see if he has picked up any fleas, ticks, or other parasites.

A dog will often scratch himself, but repeated scratching is a common sign of fleas.

Fleas

Fleas move very fast, making it hard to spot them, but you may notice the signs in flea dirt, which appears as tiny black specks. These contain the undigested remains of your pet's blood that have passed through the flea's body. To be sure the specks are flea dirt rather than mud, tip them onto a damp piece of paper towel. If they dissolve and leave a red deposit, this confirms the presence of blood. If you do spot a flea, try to grab it between your thumb and finger and drop it down the toilet to be sure that it cannot escape. If you have confirmed the presence of fleas, you will need a special flea comb to groom your dog and catch as many fleas as possible.

The best way to protect your dog from an epidemic of fleas is to treat the condition before it happens. Plenty of preventative products are available, but you need to choose one that is appropriate for your dog. For instance, one that is suitable for an older dog may not be suitable for a puppy. Ask your veterinarian if you are unsure.

Flea Control

An array of products is available to control fleas. You can purchase an over-the-counter brand, or if the problem is persistent, your veterinarian can provide you with a prescription for a stronger product. Whichever you choose, read the instructions carefully. Most are deadly to fish, so never treat your pet outside near a pond with fish, or indoors close to an aquarium—especially if you are using an aerosol type. If a flea-infested dog has been sleeping on your bed, you must strip off all the sheets and wash them. Carefully vacuum the mattress, the floor area, and under the bed. Some people are more vulnerable to fleabites than others. Most suffer bites around the ankles because fleas hatch from their pupae at the sound of movement and spring up onto this part of the body.

Flea products are usually administered in the form of a liquid drop on the back of the neck—you will need to part the fur carefully to apply the drop directly onto the skin. The ingredients are absorbed into the dog's body and circulate in the blood. That way, if a flea feeds on your dog, it will ingest the chemical. Some products kill fleas directly, while others contain an insect growth regulator (IGR), which interferes with the flea's ability to breed. Although the flea will still be able to lay eggs, the larvae will not hatch, eliminating the risk of an epidemic.

Dognosis
Staying Cool

Dogs naturally groom themselves by licking and nibbling at their coat, but they also frequently lick themselves when they are hot. They lack sweat glands; instead, the evaporation of saliva from their bodies helps them to cool down.

You are more likely to see flea dirt than the creatures themselves. However, it is usually possible to spot them on short-coated dogs, especially those with a white coat, because fleas are dark in color.

Ticks

When grooming your dog, you may also uncover ticks hidden in among the fur. These particular parasites often have complex lifecycles, and wild animals—such as deer—may play a part. Dogs acquire ticks when walking through areas where they are present—young ticks are quite mobile and readily anchor onto a dog's legs or body, especially if your pet lies down in vegetation for any length of time.

At first, ticks are small and quite hard to spot. They attach themselves using their strong mouthparts, which penetrate the dog's skin, and once they begin feeding, they soon start to swell dramatically in size. If you have not seen a tick before, you may initially fear that your pet has a skin growth of some kind. Different species of tick differ slightly in color and appearance, but if you look very closely at the point where the parasite is attached to the skin, you will spot the tick's tiny legs. (See pages 160—162.)

Fleas lay their eggs in furniture and carpets, so if your pet takes a liking to the sofa, be sure to throw a washable protective cover over it.

Grooming

Stroking your pet will help to remove loose hair from the coat, especially when your dog is molting, but many dogs require regular grooming sessions to keep their coats in good condition and prevent them from becoming matted. As well as helping to remove dead hair, brushing acts as a tonic for the skin by improving the blood flow. Once again, this is something that a dog should be accustomed to in puppyhood. In fact,

Dogs require different grooming techniques, depending in part on the length of their coat. A variety of brushes and combs is available, so choose the equipment suitable for your pet.

it is easier to groom long-coated dogs at this age, because their coats are less profuse than those of adults. Be prepared for a young dog to wriggle—you will need to encourage your pet to stand still, which is an important part of his training. Even so, it is a good idea to start grooming after a playing session so your puppy will be less excitable.

A variety of different grooming tools is available. For a short-coated dog with virtually no undercoat, such as a whippet, a light brushing with a hound glove—which has short bristles or pins on the palm—is sufficient. Dogs with longer, thicker coats will need combing as well, to prevent their fur from becoming tangled, but be careful that this is not a painful experience for your pet; otherwise, he may be difficult to groom in the future. Using a special comb with teeth that rotate will help, because these break down mats in the coat.

Be sensitive about the way you use the comb. Try to break down any matting with your fingers first rather than trying to comb it through; teasing the hair apart gently will make the grooming process less traumatic. With severe matting it may be better to cut the knots out of the dog's coat rather than trying to break them apart by grooming. Your dog will not develop knots of this type if you groom him regularly.

Dogs with long, profuse coats, such as the Afghan hound, will need daily grooming. Short-coated dogs can be groomed just once a week, although more frequently when they are molting—which has the added advantage of preventing hair from shedding around the home on carpeting or furniture. Dogs tend to molt twice a year, in spring and fall. Breeds from northern areas normally molt most heavily, losing their dense winter undercoat in spring. The owners of some long-haired breeds even collect their pet's fur, spinning it into wool to make garments.

Some dogs, mostly those with wiry coats, such as poodle breeds, terriers, and Airedales, do not shed their fur. Their coat care is therefore very different, because they need to have their hair trimmed back every six to eight weeks or so to maintain their appearance. Grooming parlors will do this, but you must decide how you want your pet's coat styled. Grooming for show purposes in breeds such as the poodles, for instance, can be very demanding—this is why those with pet poodles often opt for the much simpler lamb trim, which is also used for puppies.

Take special care when grooming around your dog's face, so that you avoid catching his eye if he moves

This young dog's fur has a wiry texture, and his coat is likely to become longer as he grows older. If you are unsure about how to groom your puppy or if his coat needs trimming, take him to a groomer.

Grooming Techniques

The way in which you groom a long-haired dog differs from the way you groom a short-haired dog. With longhairs it is better to brush the coat in the opposite direction first to remove loose hair before brushing it back down again. Finish by combing in the direction of the lie of the coat. A brush with natural bristles is better than one made with nylon bristles, because it will reduce static in the coat.

suddenly without warning. If you want to trim back any hair close to or over-hanging his eyes, use a small pair of round-ended (not sharp-tipped) scissors and a relatively small comb.

An Irish wolfhound's coat is wiry but not especially long, so grooming is straightforward. Take care to clean the hair around the mouth frequently, however, because this area tends to become soiled by food.

Hair Around the Mouth

The other area that may need cleaning is the hair around the lips, especially if you feed your dog wet food. In wire-haired breeds and those that have profuse hair around their mouth, notably bearded collies, the fur in this area may become matted and start to smell unpleasant. The immediate solution is to clean the area by washing it, although trimming back the fur or switching to a diet of dry food is a better option.

Ringworm

When grooming your dog, look out for any bald patches. This may simply be due to a skin irritation, which has caused your dog to nibble at his fur, or it may be due to the way his hair lies. Large breeds, such as the Irish wolfhound, sometimes suffer from localized hair loss for this reason. However, there could be a more sinister cause, such as ringworm. In spite of its name, this is a fungal infection, and although it is not very serious, it can cause zoonotic disease, which can spread to humans.

Ringworm is transmitted by fungal spores, which can survive for months in the environment. The infection causes red circular patches on the skin in people, usually on the forearms.

Seek veterinary advice without delay if you suspect your dog may be suffering from this disease.

Your veterinarian may be able to confirm ringworm by shining a special light, known as a Wood's lamp, onto the affected area in a darkened room. If ringworm is present, the area fluoresces a bright shade of apple green. If the light test does not confirm ringworm, further testing will be necessary to eliminate this possibility. Skin scrapings will be taken from the border of the affected area where the fungus will be most active if it is present. These will be transferred to a special cultural medium in the laboratory to see if the fungus will grow. The appropriate treatment can then be given.

Tear Staining

Some breeds, notably those with very compact faces, such as the Pekingese, pug, or Maltese, may suffer from tear staining running down their cheeks near the nose. This is because of a deviation of the tear gland, which would normally drain the tear fluid away into the nostrils but instead allows it to overflow out of the inner corner of each eye. Wipe the staining away with a damp cotton ball, although for a long-term solution, surgery can be done to improve the drainage.

Getting Cozy

You will find it easier to establish a bond with your puppy if you allow him to sit and sleep on a sofa, but if you want your dog to remain on the floor, you must make this clear from the outset. It will be virtually impossible to break this habit at a later stage when your dog is older.

However, it is better not to allow small dogs such as dachshunds to jump up onto furnishings or into a car, because of their susceptibility to intervertebral disk problems. If you do allow your dog on the sofa, you can prevent it from being covered in dog hair by using a throw or thick blanket, which can be purchased from dog bed suppliers. A throw will also protect the cushions—some dogs scratch at the cushions before settling down. This is instinctive behavior—a wild dog will scrape at the ground to remove any stones and create a more comfortable hollow before settling down to sleep.

Even if your dog is allowed on a chair, he will also need a bed because there will be times when he prefers to sleep there instead. A wide range of dog beds is now available. Choose a design that is fully washable, because even if

A Dog's Tale
Sleeping preferences

Some breeds of dog instinctively seek out warm places in which to sleep. For instance, those with thin coats, such as the whippet, or hairless dogs, such as the Mexican hairless, often prefer to burrow beneath covers. If you buy a double-layered blanket, held together with a zipper, your dog will soon learn to snuggle down inside it, using it like a sleeping bag. He will adjust his position if he becomes too hot.

your dog does not suffer from fleas, he will inevitably leave hair on his bed, especially when molting. Regular washing is also important to prevent the material from acquiring a distinctive doggy odor.

A dog's bed will provide your pet with his own space, and a variety of styles is available. Wicker designs, such as this one, are not recommended for young puppies, however, because they are tempted to chew them, which may cause choking.

Bathing Your Dog

Your dog may enjoy getting as dirty as this but a bath is not always necessary. Simply wait until the mud dries, and brush it out.

Most dogs need a bath about four to six times a year in order to curb any unpleasant body odor. Once again, it is helpful to start this with a young dog so that later in life baths will not frighten him.

Show dogs tend to be bathed more frequently than their pet counterparts, so they are often dried thoroughly with a hair dryer. This can be a frightening experience, so again it is something that your dog needs to become accustomed to from an early age.

Start with the hair dryer on a low setting so it is neither noisy nor blasting out air, ensuring the air temperature is slightly warm rather than hot. Hold the dryer away from the head and run your hands through the coat as you work so the air can penetrate the fur easily, speeding up the drying process.

A Clean Dog Is Not Always a Happy Dog
A pungent doggy odor may be unpleasant to us, but it is important to your pet. When taking your dog out for a walk after giving him a bath, you will need to be careful at first, because he will probably try to find something smelly to roll in, such as cow or fox excrement. This will inevitably mean that you have to bathe him again without delay—and you will also need to wash the blanket or cushion used to line his traveling crate if you have traveled to the walk by car.

No Need for a Bath!
If you have a longhaired dog, do not worry too much when he comes back muddy after a walk. It is not necessary to wash your dog to remove mud; simply towel off as much as possible and then wait for the remainder to dry. At that later stage you can easily brush it out of your pet's coat without any problem.

Step-by-Step Guide to Bathing Your Dog

Do not use your own bath or shower area for washing a dog—not just on grounds of hygiene, but also because if your pet becomes distressed and struggles, he may scratch the base with his claws. It is much better to bathe your dog outdoors anyway, because it tends to be a fairly messy task. Before you begin, take off your dog's collar. If he struggles while being washed, you may find it helpful to use a nylon collar in the bath instead to make it easier to control him.

Step 1 If your dog is small enough, you may be able to use a plastic baby bath in which to wash him. Otherwise, you will have to find something larger or wash him standing outside in the backyard, providing he's tethered somehow and not able just to run away. You will also need a clean bucket or jug, a plastic cup, an old towel, and a canine shampoo.

Step 2 Begin by filling the jug with tepid water and pouring some of this into the bath. Then carefully lift your dog into the bath, giving him plenty of reassurance. Start to wet his legs, using your hand to bale the water up over his body. He may not like this and try to leap out, but you must keep him under control.

Step 3 Use the jug to pour water over his back, moving from his hindquarters toward his head and stopping at his neck. Most dogs will allow their body to be soaked with water, but they often resent their head being wet, so leave this until last.

Step 4 Work the shampoo into your dog's coat just as if you were washing your own hair. Create a lather, taking great care to avoid his eyes. It may be better to wipe his face with a moist towel rather than trying to shampoo it at all.

Step 5 Rinse the shampoo out thoroughly by pouring clean water from the jug over the soapy areas. If your dog is reasonably cooperative, you may be able to use a hose on low power instead, which is more effective, although it is not ideal to use cold water.

Step 6 When you have finished rinsing off your dog's coat, lift him out of the bath and stand back. The first thing he will do is shake his body vigorously to remove as much water as possible from his coat. Afterward, call him to you, throw a towel over him, and take him indoors so you can dry his fur off to prevent him from developing a chill.

111

Ears, Claws, and Teeth

Ear Care

Most of the time you will not need to worry about cleaning your dog's ears. However, spaniels are susceptible to problems because of the way their heavy ears hang down over the ear canal. The warm, humid conditions thus created predispose the breed to localized bacterial or fungal infections, and ear mites may also become established. The resulting irritation will cause the dog to start scratching repeatedly at his ears. The problem must be dealt with immediately or the earflap may be damaged. The trauma of constant scratching may also result in internal bleeding, giving rise to a hematoma, which will cause the earflap to become noticeably swollen.

A long-action flea treatment may also control ear mites, but it will not curb bacteria or fungi. For these you will need a specific treatment from your vet, which must be given as instructed to cure the problem. Along with the treatment it is a good idea to trim back the hair on the inner

Spaniels have heavy ears, which makes them susceptible to ear infections. Repeated scratching around the ears is an early indicator of such a problem.

surface of the ears so it cannot mat over the entrance to the ear canal. Do not be tempted to stop treatment early because your dog appears to have recovered and is no longer scratching. The infection could still be there and may become chronic, requiring surgery to open up the ear canal.

Pedicures

Check your dog's claws regularly to ensure they have not become overgrown; the most likely to cause a problem are the dewclaws, which are usually located on the inner sides of each foot. They are not subjected to normal wear since they are not in contact with the ground, so they may begin to curl around into the pads if their growth is not kept in check.

Special clippers are available to keep your pet's claws trimmed, although your vet will carry out this task. Never cut the nail too short, because it will bleed. In dogs with light-colored claws, you will be able to see the "quick" as a pinkish area extending out from each toe, which marks the area of live nail. You need to cut away from this into the clear area of dead tissue. Guillotine-type clippers are the easiest to use because you can position the nail accurately in place before trimming off the tip. In dogs with black claws, it is much harder to ascertain the position of the "quick," so the help of a veterinarian is beneficial.

If your dog starts limping, beware of examining his feet too closely, because the associated pain may cause him to snap at you.

Paws for Concern

In some cases—notably in the late summer—your dog's feet may become severely irritated, causing him constantly to bite and nibble at them. The reason is likely to be the presence of tiny harvest mite larvae (*Trombicula*) that your dog has picked up when out walking. They are almost impossible to see with the naked eye and you will need to be careful if you try to examine your dog's paws, because they may be painful. Even a friendly, docile pet may become short-tempered and snap at you.

The simplest treatment for harvest mite larvae is to mix up a solution of a suitable medication to kill them. The problem may have other causes, however, such as a grass seed that has penetrated between the paws. This will also be very painful, and your dog may even limp. A veterinary checkup should be carried out to establish the exact cause; your dog can be sedated if necessary so that a proper examination can be carried out and appropriate treatment given.

Dental Care

Dogs may suffer later in life from dental problems due to the buildup of tartar around the base of the teeth. This causes inflammation of the gum line, which starts to erode, loosening the teeth in their sockets. Bacteria then gain access, resulting in a painful abscess. It is therefore a good idea to train a puppy to accept having his teeth brushed regularly, which will help to prevent tartar from building up. There are special brushes and canine toothpaste available for this—human toothpaste should not be used, because its ingredients are not suitable. Open your pet's mouth and gently brush the teeth. A puppy is likely to struggle at first but will soon come to accept this as part of his regular grooming care. Dry food can help to prevent tartar buildup, and some of these foods contain special ingredients to aid dental care. It is also more pleasant for you if your pet's teeth are polished, because it will ensure cleaner-smelling breath.

Dental care is very important for dogs, yet relatively few owners actually clean their dog's teeth. Special kits are available for this purpose.

Age Concerns

As dogs grow older, their behavior changes. You may notice that your pet starts to become less responsive. This is often due to a decline in their hearing.

Stroking and grooming your dog can be vital to his health as he grows older. Be alert for any swellings under the coat, which could indicate a skin growth. Your veterinarian should always check these, although growths are often benign tumors similar to warts. They can usually be removed surgically, especially if spotted at an early stage, but unfortunately they often regrow. Changes on the earflaps, particularly in pale-coated dogs, can be more concerning, because this is a common part of the body for skin tumors known as melanomas to appear. They are usually triggered by prolonged exposure to the sun's ultraviolet rays, and there are special preventative creams for dogs that you can apply, especially if your dog spends much of his time outdoors.

As your pet grows older, you will notice some change in the coloration of his coat, particularly if he has a dark-colored muzzle. The color here is likely to fade, becoming grayish, although the rest of the coat will probably remain black. There is nothing that can be done to reverse this change in coloration.

Mobility
Inevitably, your pet's energy level is likely to decline with age. However, an inability to run or move as freely as he did in the past could be the result of a serious condition. It is always best to check with your veterinarian if you have any concerns, especially if your dog's lack of enthusiasm comes on suddenly.

Fly Strike
With age, your dog may have difficulty relieving himself easily, thus causing his fur to become soiled—particularly

if he is a long-haired breed. Check this area regularly and be prepared to trim the coat and wash off any affected places. This is especially important in hot weather because flies may be attracted to the soiled areas of the coat and lay their eggs there, which hatch rapidly into maggots. These then burrow into the skin beneath, with potentially deadly consequences for your dog because the maggots release a toxin that is carried via the bloodstream through the dog's body, affecting vital organs, including the heart. If your pet's heart is already weak for any reason, the outcome can be fatal.

If you discover your pet has been affected by fly strike, use a pair of blunt-ended tweezers to remove the maggots immediately, then cut away the hair and clean the affected area. Your vet will be able to monitor your dog's condition and give you wound powder to aid the healing process.

Joint Pain

Older dogs can suffer from painful joints due to arthritis. The hip joints are often affected, particularly in larger dogs. You may notice that your dog appears stiff when he first wakes up, although he should be walking normally soon afterward.

He may also find it difficult to jump up, particularly into the back of a vehicle. Beware of lifting him, because he may snap at you unexpectedly due to the pain when you try to pick him up. Instead,

Dietary Supplements

If your dog is suffering from painful joints, you can supplement his diet with compounds known as chondroprotectants. These aid production of the cartilage that lines joints and can stimulate blood flow; the cartilage acts as a covering, protecting the bone in the joints. Chondroprotectants include both glucosamine and chondroitin, and these chemicals may be combined with other components, such as manganese and ascorbate, which are called nutraceuticals—dietary ingredients that will directly benefit your dog's health. Some pet-food manufacturers now add these components to their senior diets as a matter of course. Extracts of the New Zealand green-lipped mussel (*Perna canaliculus*) are also often added in supplements of this type—they contain glycosaminoglycan and other potentially beneficial compounds, such as omega-3 fatty acids.

purchase a special ramp so your dog can easily walk up into your vehicle.

There is little that can be done to cure painful joints, but you can alleviate the symptoms so they are less troublesome for your pet. Start by having a thorough veterinary examination to ascertain the extent of the problem. Your vet may prescribe

Large dogs, such as the German shepherd, often experience painful hip joints. Other breeds can be vulnerable to joint pain in the vicinity of the neck.

painkillers, but be aware that these will mask the signs of pain and you must not encourage your pet to overexert himself, because this will be counterproductive—the aim is to find a balance. It may be a matter of taking your dog on a series of shorter walks rather than on one long one so he doesn't get overtired but has the same amount of exercise. You do not want him to start putting on more weight, because this will place the joints under more strain—in fact, if your pet is already overweight, putting him on a diet will help.

Other treatments that can be useful include acupuncture, which can be very effective at blocking the pain. It may even allow you to dispense with medication for your

pet, although again it does not provide a cure. If you want to try this, ask your vet to refer you to a practitioner. Some pet health insurance policies may cover some—if not all—of the cost of this treatment.

Physiotherapy is another option. This may help an older dog that is suffering from joint pain, as well as benefiting a dog that has pulled a muscle or been injured in some way. A course of treatment can help a dog to recover a full range of movement and build up muscle strength. Again, your vet will be able to refer you to a specialist. To aid your pet's recovery, it is often a good idea to continue some of the exercises at home. So be prepared to do this, once the physiotherapist has shown you what is required.

You can keep your dog active in old age by taking him for regular hydrotherapy sessions. The water will support his weight, helping to overcome the pain of arthritic joints.

Body Fitness

If a dog is not receiving regular exercise because of a musculoskeletal problem, his muscles will tend to atrophy and become weaker, and his overall level of fitness will decline. The best thing you can do to help your pet under these circumstances is take him swimming—the water will support his weight so his joints are no longer bearing it, removing much of the pain associated with osteoarthritis, for example. A dog will often feel comfortable swimming, even if just before entering the water he has been reluctant to walk any distance, let alone run. However, if your dog has other health issues, such as a heart problem, it is very important to follow veterinary advice on the length of time he should be allowed to swim.

You do not need a stretch of water near you to take your pet swimming—in fact, this may be dangerous if it is polluted, the currents are strong, or the water is cold. Instead, your vet will probably be able to refer you to a canine hydrotherapy center, where your pet will be constantly supervised in temperature-controlled water and where he can be carefully dried off afterward before going home. Several sessions will be needed for the benefits to become apparent, because it will take time to build up his muscle tone.

Your dog may be nervous at first, especially if he has not swum before and does not belong to a breed with a history of working in water, but he will soon look forward to these sessions.

Dogs of all ages enjoy swimming, particularly those bred to work in water, although those with thin coats are usually less inclined to take the plunge.

Equipment for Leg Ailments

A whole range of equipment can help with joint injuries arising from old age or following an accident, although much depends on the precise nature of your dog's injury. A harness around the hindquarters that will allow you to support your dog when he is standing, if this part of the body is weak, can be very useful. Slings of this type are available in different sizes. There are also carts on wheels to aid a dog's mobility if the hindlimbs are affected—these can be useful both in cases of temporary disability and for permanent paralysis. Dogs usually adjust quickly to walking with their hind legs supported by a cart, but you will have to supervise your pet more closely, especially in public areas such as parks, where he will encounter other dogs.

Social Senses

Domestic dogs are social animals by nature, which helps them bond with us, but they also comprise all of the key elements of communication held by their ancestor, the gray wolf. In certain respects their senses are actually superior to ours, so we have come to rely on a number of these talents, and as a result, dogs have become valuable working companions.

A Dog's Bark

The sound of a dog's bark can be audible from a considerable distance, especially at night, when there is less traffic and other background noise.

One of the most obvious ways dogs have adapted to domestication is the way they bark. Wolves—even those living in packs—are much quieter by nature, since they do not want to draw close attention to their presence in a region. This relative silence is not necessarily because of fear of people, but more because making noise might encourage invasions into their territory by neighboring packs. Wolves will most likely howl from dusk onward, when they are less conspicuous, and tracking down their position will be harder than during the day.

However, to humans one of the obvious advantages of keeping dogs is their ability to detect danger—especially at nighttime, when it is dark. As a result, from the time dogs were first domesticated, they were encouraged to bark and warn of any threat. This characteristic is still very evident today—mainly in breeds that were developed as guardians, such as rottweilers. Barking appears to be a trait that has been modified extensively through domestication and selective breeding. While a number of hunting dogs seek their quarry without barking so they won't betray their presence, scent hounds will bay loudly when following a trail.

Different Tones
The domestic dog's bark is usually very different from the sound of a wolf: It is a shorter yet more intense

Dognosis
A Personal Sound

Even with two dogs of the same breed, it is very likely that you will notice a slight difference in the sound of their voices—especially when they are barking—which allows you to tell them apart. Similarly, wolves that become separated are able to distinguish between pack members by the sound of their calls.

rare in their New Guinea homeland, these dogs are currently being bred in some countries, including the United States.

In contrast, the basenji, a breed that reached the West from the vicinity of the African Congo, is sometimes described as the barkless dog. It has been suggested that the quiet nature of these dogs arose because they were traditionally used as hunting companions, so their stealth behavior was a vital attribute. Basenjis can utter calls that sound similar to yodeling, particularly when they are excited.

The basenji, traditionally used as a hunting companion, is sometimes called the barkless dog because of its quiet nature.

aggressive sound. However, the breeds that retain the strongest similarity to wolves in their physical appearance—such as the Siberian husky—bark in a way that is strongly reminiscent of howling.

In Southeast Asia pariah dogs— dogs that have lived closely with people but have reverted to a more free-living existence—will bark collectively, which is another very wolflike trait. The best-known pariah dog, the New Guinea singing dog— considered to be a close relative of Australia's dingo—gets its name from the way it barks: Its calls have an attractive musical quality. When one of these dogs starts barking, others of the group in the neighborhood join in, starting a chorus that reflects the way members of a wolf pack may respond to the calls of a companion. Although they are now apparently

Hearing

Dogs generally are more sensitive to sound than people are, and their hearing range is much wider than ours. However, like people, a dog's hearing will decline with age—gundogs especially due to the loud bangs they are subjected to while working.

Wolves will howl to keep in touch with each other, particularly at night. Howling also warns neighboring packs not to invade their territory.

Most German shepherds have floppy ears when they are born, but within six months their ears turn upright, resembling those of a wolf.

Ear Shape

There may also be some differences in the hearing abilities of different breeds, based on the shape of their ears. Certain breeds, such as the German shepherd, are characterized partly by their triangular upright ears, which resemble those of wolves. These ears can be moved slightly with special muscles, allowing the source of the sound to be pinpointed accurately. In some cases, such as with whippets, the ears are flexible enough to lie back along the head but still be raised when the dog is alert.

Many scent hounds and hunting dogs have ears that hang down the sides of the head. This does not seriously impair their hearing, and it has the benefit of protecting the sensitive inner part of the ear from being injured by sharp branches or thorns as they run through undergrowth. It does, however, have some impact on the dog's body language, because the range of possible movements is significantly reduced, so the ears play a less important role (see page 92). In wolves raised ears are a sign of assertion, and floppy ears are a feature seen only in young wolf cubs. This applies to puppies, too—young German shepherds have floppy ears,

Dognosis
Hearing Secret Harmonies

The typical hearing range of a dog extends from 20 hertz up to 100,000—the upper limit of our hearing range reaches only about 20,000 hertz. This enables dogs to hear the sounds of rodent prey— inaudible to our ears—in the ultrasound part of the hearing spectrum. It also explains why dog whistles that we cannot hear can clearly be heard from afar by dogs.

which usually develop into pricked ears by the time they are six months old, although in some cases neither of the ears, or only one ear, will become raised.

Deafness and Behavior

Congenital deafness is a problem found in some dogs, notably white boxers and white English bull terriers. The dog may appear unresponsive, although he will compensate as much as possible, relying to a much greater degree on eyesight. It is often very difficult to test whether a dog is deaf, because if you simply clap your hands near your dog's head, the resulting air currents will reverberate across his fur, attracting his attention even if he did not hear the noise.

Unfortunately, there is no treatment for congenital deafness. You will need to be very careful when exercising your dog near roads, because he will not hear approaching traffic or your calls. Following a set routine is important to give him confidence. You'll also find that hand signals will play a more significant part in the training process. Think ahead when approaching your pet, especially if he is nervous, because you may frighten him if you approach him from behind or when he is dozing. He will not be able to hear you and might react aggressively.

Sight

A dog's reliance on his sense of sight, both for information about his

A Dog's Tale
Fields of Vision

It's hard to creep undetected past a sighthound such as a borzoi. They can see better than other dogs, thanks to the positioning of the eyes on the sides of their heads and their elongated, narrow faces. This means they can see about 270 degrees out of the maximum of the 360 degree circle around the head. Round-headed breeds, such as the Boston terrier, whose eyes are located more centrally in the skull, have a field of vision of 200 degrees, while by comparison, our field of vision is limited to 100 degrees.

Long, trailing ears protect sensitive inner parts of the ear from injury.

environment and for communication, is another characteristic affected by selective breeding. The way dogs perceive the world differs from our view of it. Although dogs can see in color, this ability is not strongly developed, because of the respective numbers of the two types of cell that comprise the retina at the back of each eye, where the image is formed. Color vision depends on cones, which respond most effectively under bright lighting conditions. Dogs have a higher proportion of rod cells than cones, however, which function better when the light is low, and this gives them better nighttime vision than humans. They also have a mechanism that boosts their ability to see under poor lighting conditions: Behind the retina there is a reflective layer, the *tapetum lucidum*, which acts like a mirror, reflecting back rays of light that have passed through this part of the eye. This ensures that the maximum possible amount of light reaches the retina, helping to reinforce the image. This is also the reason why dogs' eyes appear to glow in the dark when a light is shone directly at them.

Coping with Loss of Vision

Some inherited conditions, most notably progressive retinal atrophy (PRA), can cause dogs to go blind at a relatively early age. This is one reason why it is important to have breeding stock checked as far back as possible. Many older canines also develop cataracts, which will impair their vision.

However, dogs adapt much better to blindness than humans do, simply because they are less dependent on their sense of sight. In familiar surroundings a blind dog is usually able to find its way around in relative safety without bumping into furniture or otherwise hurting himself. This is partly because he knows the layout of the room, but also because his hearing and sense of smell help him avoid obstacles nearby. Talking to a blind dog frequently will help him to orientate toward the sound of your voice. It is very important to take special care when exercising a blind dog to keep him out of danger.

Dogs have keen eyesight, which helps them to coordinate their movements—as demonstrated by this spaniel jumping up to catch a flying disk in midair.

Scenting Skills

Scent provides an important medium for dogs to communicate with each other. Wolf packs mark the borders of their territory repeatedly with their urine to indicate their presence, and in a similar way, male dogs use their urine to mark trees and lampposts or other prominent sites. The urine is projected onto a vertical surface, at what is likely to be the height of a dog's head, so it is very conspicuous to other dogs passing by. Dogs usually do not behave this way indoors, because they view this as their "den" area. If an adult dog scents indoors, it is usually indicative of a behavioral or medical problem (see page 180).

Dogs not only distinguish other animals by their scent, they can also determine just how recently the other dog passed by—as well as gleaning other information, such as if the other dog has been neutered. A male dog will attempt to urinate frequently in different spots to mark his scent when out on a walk, until there is no urine left—although if undeterred, he may still continue cocking his leg. This is normal behavior, particularly in an area where dogs are commonly walked, and it does not indicate a urinary tract problem, such as cystitis. However, if your dog's bladder is full, he will simply relieve himself at the earliest opportunity.

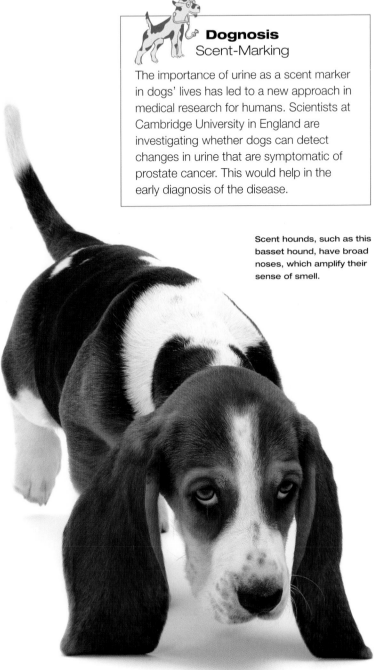

Dognosis
Scent-Marking

The importance of urine as a scent marker in dogs' lives has led to a new approach in medical research for humans. Scientists at Cambridge University in England are investigating whether dogs can detect changes in urine that are symptomatic of prostate cancer. This would help in the early diagnosis of the disease.

Scent hounds, such as this basset hound, have broad noses, which amplify their sense of smell.

Other Scents

Sweat provides another way for dogs to leave a scent, especially since their only sweat glands are located between their toes. However, our restricted sense of smell means that you will not notice that your dog has sweaty feet! The most obvious sign of scent marking with sweat occurs after defecation, when your dog will scratch repeatedly at the ground nearby. This also provides a distinctive visual marking, which other dogs will recognize and sniff to identify the animal responsible. A pair of anal "glands" is located within the rectum, just before the anal opening itself. These produce a potent secretion that is transferred to the feces every time a dog defecates. The pungent scent also explains why dogs are so eager to sniff the anogenital region when they meet. There also may be a slight secretion of fluid from the sacs, reinforcing the scent.

The dog's acute sense of smell is particularly noticeable when there is a bitch in heat nearby. It is definitely not a good idea to take a bitch out for a walk in this condition, because she is likely to attract a host of male dogs from all around the neighborhood.

The bitch produces chemical attractants, known as pheromones, at this stage in her reproductive cycle, and these waft on air currents over considerable distances. In addition to detecting scents with their nose, dogs have another olfactory organ, situated in the roof of the mouth. This is known as the vomeronasal, or Jacobson's, organ, and it connects

Dognosis
Raised Legs

Male dogs start to cock their hind leg when urinating once they have attained sexual maturity, typically at six to eight months old. Until then they will urinate the same way as a bitch, by squatting down on the ground. A male dog who has been neutered after maturity may continue to urinate by cocking his leg on occasion, but he is likely to revert to squatting frequently as well. Bitches may occasionally lift one of their hind legs when urinating, but they very rarely cock their leg.

directly to the area of the brain concerned with mating behavior. Pheromones may trigger this part of the dog's olfactory system rather than registering primarily via the nasal cavities.

A Wet Nose

Dogs generally have moist noses, with fluid draining down from glands in the nose. Your dog can also lick his nose to keep it moist. This is important because moisture improves a dog's scenting skills. The nostrils are very flexible—the slits at the sides mean that dogs can flare their nostrils, drawing in more air when they inhale and potentially more scent molecules.

The shape of a dog's nose helps indicate if a breed is likely to be a talented tracker. Many breeds of French origin are good tracker dogs—the best known is probably the basset hound, but there is also the grand bleu de Gascoigne. Both breeds have a family resemblance to the bloodhound, an ancient breed that was probably the original ancestor of most scent-hound stock. The bloodhound was known originally in Europe as the Saint Hubert hound.

A Sense of Smell

Some dogs have a more acute sense of smell than others. Scent hounds are the most talented in this respect: They have much larger noses, which is apparent if you compare the facial

A Dog's Tale On the Scent
Stories of using bloodhounds to track down escaped prisoners are almost legendary. These scent hounds have been known to follow "cold trails" left by people more than four days before, and their stamina is so strong that they can continue to track for over 100 miles (160 km). Other types of dog, including retrievers and spaniels, can also be trained to pick up individual scents. As a result, they may be employed for a variety of other law-enforcement tasks, such as seeking out drug smugglers or explosives.

profiles of a bloodhound and a sight hound, such as a greyhound. Breeds with very short, compact muzzles, such as the pug and Pekingese, are the least talented at detecting scents. A long, broad nose helps ensure that a higher percentage of scent molecules stays within the nasal cavity, while the

Moisture improves a dog's scenting ability, and one way a dog keeps its nose moist is by using its muscular tongue.

Breeds with very short noses, such as pugs, are more prone to heat stroke than those with larger noses, because their nasal cavities are so small. The evaporation of moisture from the cavity normally helps a dog to stay cool.

turbinates—the mesh of fine scrolls of bone inside the nose—greatly increase the surface area for scent detection.

Dogs have a sense of smell that may be many million times better than our own—some breeds possess as many as 220 million cells to detect scents in their noses, while we have just 5 million. Although the dog's scenting skills have been enhanced by domestication, wolves also rely heavily on this ability to locate their quarry and can pick up the scent of deer from a 1.5-mile (2.4-km) distance.

However, the scenting ability of dogs is not consistent, and it can be

A Dog's Tale
The History of the Saint Bernard

The type of dog most associated with finding people is the Saint Bernard, a breed of mastiff descent created at the Bernardine Hospice high in the Swiss Alps and named after the founder of the order, Bernard de Mentho. The hospice was near an important pass through the mountains, and in winter travelers often became lost in the blizzards that swept through the region. Large mastiff-type dogs had been kept locally since Roman times, but in the 18th century the monks started to crossbreed these dogs with great Danes to create animals with better scenting skills to locate stranded travelers.

The Saint Bernard breed is credited with saving more than 2,000 lives over the course of two centuries. The most famous dog so far is a male named Barry who rescued 40 people between 1800 and 1812. For a period afterward the breed became known as the Barry dog, and Barry, who died in 1814, can still be seen—thanks to a taxidermist's skill—at Bern's Museum of Natural History, close to where he lived.

The Saint Bernard really caught the public imagination in the late 1800s because of a famous painting by Victorian artist Sir Edwin Landseer. His picture depicted these dogs wearing

The story of the Saint Bernard carrying brandy has no basis in fact.

small kegs of brandy on their collars to revive travelers suffering from cold. The power of the painting was so strong that this became widely accepted as fact, but it was simply artistic license.

affected by various factors. These include age, since puppies have a more limited sense of smell than adult dogs. Also—not surprisingly—if a dog is hungry, his ability to detect a scent increases; after eating a fatty meal, this skill declines.

A Nose for Danger

The scenting ability of the dog has been harnessed in various ways, helping to keep us safe. Dogs have been trained to seek out explosives, find people buried in earthquakes, and locate lost travelers. Scent hounds, however, are not often used for this purpose—they are better

equipped to follow a trail on their own rather than to work closely with people. Instead, hunting-dog breeds, such as retrievers and spaniels, are favored for this type of work because they are used to distinguishing scents, working closely on a one-to-one basis with their handlers, and are generally more responsive.

Extra Odor

The natural scent of a dog means that most breeds will require bathing every two or three months before the smell becomes unpleasant around the home—particularly in wet weather. Unfortunately, many dogs

Coat texture varies between individual dogs. Those with long or wiry coats are better protected when working in the undergrowth than sleek-coated dogs with virtually no undercoat.

The pointer is known for its classic stance when alerting his handler to the presence of quarry nearby. Even pet pointers may instinctively behave in this fashion.

do not appreciate their owners' efforts to keep them sweet smelling! If you take your pet walking in a rural area soon after a bath, you may find that he will seek out strong-smelling materials to roll in. Cow pies are a favorite, but sheep or goat dung may be selected as well.

It is sometimes suggested that this habit mimics the hunting behavior of wolves because rolling in dung helps the wolf mask his scent when hunting. There is no real evidence for this, however. It seems more likely that a dog's rolling behavior is triggered by a need to enhance his social status

with a strong odor after a bath has removed his own scent. The strong smell certainly appears to arouse the curiosity of other dogs they may subsequently meet.

Working Dogs

The characteristics of some breeds have been developed to aid them as working dogs. These traits are often refinements of the wolf's hunting behavior. The baying call of the bloodhound indicates when these hounds are on the trail of their quarry, but hunting dogs communicate this information to their handlers differently because it could be disadvantageous to alert the quarry to the hunter's presence.

Pointers, for instance, adopt a very distinctive posture when they detect the scent of prey. They stand with their nose erect and a front foot lifted off the ground, pointing in the direction of the scent—although they obviously cannot indicate the distance of the target. This posture is called the point. The way that pointers stand frozen is part of their ancestors' hunting ritual, because wolves also stand motionless for a few moments after picking up the scent of their prey.

Sitting for Prey

Another aspect of the wolf's hunting behavior is demonstrated in some breeds of setter, whose name comes from the old English verb "to set," which means "to sit." When a setter has detected his quarry, he will sit down; members of a wolf pack will also pause to observe their target rather than give chase immediately. Setters have given rise to the spaniel lineage—a group of smaller breeds that are also kept as hunting dogs. Spaniels will expose game rather than simply indicate its close presence.

Hunter-Gatherers

Even the behavior of retrievers mimics a behavior pattern seen in wolves, who will instinctively return with food to other members of the pack. This behavior is not only seen

Dogs have an innate instinct to retrieve, which is why, from an early age, your pet will quickly learn to bring a ball back to you.

when there are young wolves in the pack—old or injured animals no longer able to hunt effectively may also be assisted by other pack members.

Out and About

A dog's natural instincts can attract him to danger even when you are out together. For instance, retrievers readily take to water, so they may plunge in even if it is dangerous due to pollution, a strong current, or stormy weather.

Another hazard can be farm stock, especially sheep. Domestic dogs have a mixed relationship with these herbivores, which are the natural prey of wolves. Ironically, the domestic dog was trained as a protector of sheep early in the domestication process, either to guard or herd the flock. Flock guardians were larger than their herding counterparts, whose role was simply to move the sheep. In

Some breeds, such as the dalmatian (above), have a far more athletic build than others, such as the Cardigan Welsh corgi (right).

Hungary, for example, the komondor simply watched over the flocks, while the smaller puli breed was responsible for herding. Many breeds were created for this purpose throughout Europe: The bergamasco has a tousled white coat resembling a sheep's coat and was equipped with a sharp, spiked collar to have an advantage in combat when defending the flock against a pack of wolves.

The instinctive desire to hunt is still a part of the psyche of many dogs, which helps explain cases of sheep chasing. Particularly during the lambing period, groups of dogs may start to behave like packs of wolves—hunting down and killing young animals. Always take great care with your dog if you encounter sheep when out walking—put him on a leash, especially if you have to walk through a field of sheep. Even if the dog mostly ignores them, the presence of a strange dog can be enough to create panic in a flock of lambing ewes, resulting in premature births.

Size Doesn't Matter

Size does not usually indicate whether a dog will be drawn to farm stock. Corgis, for example, were bred as cattle dogs, trained to nip at the heels of the cows to keep a herd moving. Their small stature provided some protection from flailing hooves. Cattle are potentially dangerous animals, to you as well as your dog, so take care when out walking to be sure they are a safe distance away.

A Dog's Tale
A Dog in Wolf's Clothing

It may seem strange, but the way sheepdogs work mimics how wolves close in on their prey. The basis of this technique can easily be missed because it relies on how the dog looks at the sheep, fixing them with his gaze. In the wild members of a wolf pack work collectively to outwit their prey and make a kill. Some members of the pack show themselves, channeling the prey toward their hidden companions, who are waiting to launch an ambush. A sheepdog moves around the sheep to prevent any from breaking free, steering them in the required direction. At intervals the dog drops to the ground, not taking his eyes off the flock. Based on the distance between the dog's position and their own, the sheep instinctively sense that they are in no immediate danger, so instead of running away, they look at the dog, creating a standoff.

A working sheepdog generally operates alone and is directed by the shepherd. This relationship is crucial—just as the wild wolf-pack leader directs the pack, the shepherd instructs the dog. The dog will follow any role that a member of a wolf pack would adopt, circling around the flock or driving them forward. This type of understanding calls for a high degree of canine intelligence, so it is not surprising that sheepdogs are ranked among the most intelligent breeds. However, their intense desire to work, combined with their intelligence, means they are not well suited to a sedentary life as a domestic pet—often acting destructively out of boredom.

Intuitive Powers

There is plenty of evidence to support the fact that dogs are more sensitive to their surroundings than we are and that they are able to detect potential dangers more easily because of their finely tuned senses. This most likely explains the mysterious link between dogs and the supernatural that has shaped much of the folklore across the world.

Man's Best Friend

A dog's loyalty toward his master is not a new concept; this characteristic has been ascribed to dogs for centuries. In ancient Greece the writer Pliny recorded a remarkable early example of such behavior in the tale of a man who was murdered by his servant. After the death was discovered, a crowd soon gathered—including the servant, who seemed overcome by grief at the sight of his master's body. However, the man's dog turned on the servant and pinned him to the ground, howling in such a mournful way that those present could only describe it as the sound of grief. This vital clue helped to unmask the servant as the murderer.

This image of trust and devotion between owner and dog has never wavered through the centuries. A later story from France—which is rather similar to Pliny's tale—confirms the bond between dog and owner lasting even beyond the grave. Aubri de Montdidier, a French nobleman, was murdered by his friend Macaire while they were out hunting together at Montargis, but de Montdidier's loyal hound led another friend of his master's to the hidden grave. After the hound was taken back to the court, every time he encountered Macaire he became very aggressive toward him and had to be dragged away.

This, combined with the discovery of de Montdidier's murder, became the talk of the court, and the matter attracted the attention of King Charles VI. He ordered Macaire and the hound to be brought before him, and again the hound attempted to seize the murderer. The king decided that the matter be resolved by Ordeal of Battle, which was a common way of settling disputes at that time. Macaire armed himself with a wooden club, while the hound was provided with a shelter, and man and dog fought to the death. Macaire's leather armor afforded him some protection, but he lost concentration momentarily and the hound seized him by the throat. Just before he died from his wounds, Macaire admitted the murder.

Medieval Times

The bond between dogs and their owners continued throughout the

An Ancient Discovery

Fido is one of the most popular names for a dog, and it has ancient origins. The Latin word "fido" means "trust." Depictions of dogs, including mosaics, have been found among the ruins of Pompeii.

Together people and dogs have been able to explore and live in surroundings that might otherwise have been impossible.

medieval period in Europe. Evidence of this can still be seen today: Many effigies on carved tombs of the era, inside the great cathedrals and churches, portray women and children with small dogs at their feet.

The loyalty of dogs was tested on the battlefield, too, where they were regularly used in combat. Stories of their bravery and heroism abound: At the battle of Agincourt in 1415, for example, an English knight, Sir Peers Legh, was killed in bitter fighting, but his mastiff remained on guard until

Dognosis
Finding Their Way

Dogs are adept at finding their way back and forth in their home environment. Further afield they utilize the Earth's magnetic field to orientate themselves, as well as rely on their scenting skills. Once they are closer to home, they use their eyesight to pick out familiar landmarks.

his body could be taken away from the scene of the conflict. This dog was then taken back to the knight's home, Lyme Hall in the English county of Cheshire, and she is said to have

founded the famous bloodline—Lyme Hall mastiffs—which has continued through to the present day.

Modern Heroism

There are also many accounts of canine heroism in the 20th century, especially during the two world wars. A special award, the Dicken medal, was even instituted to commemorate animal bravery.

The first recipient of this medal was Bob, a Labrador-collie cross, who served in North Africa with the British army during the Second World War. Camouflaged in black to hide his white fur, he would alert his patrol to danger when they were behind enemy lines. He did this by standing still and refusing to move, without making a sound. On one occasion, after a short time, seeing no obvious sign of the enemy, the officer in charge ordered the men to move on, but Bob remained rooted to the spot. Then, just as they prepared to set off, the men spotted a group of enemy soldiers ahead, and thanks to Bob's instinct, they were able to retreat safely under cover of darkness.

Wolves and Dogs

It is interesting that while dogs are perceived as loyal and trusted companions, their immediate

Opposite: This illustration, which appeared in the 1917 French publication *La Baionnette*, shows a dog accompanying French soldiers out of the trenches in an attack on German lines, perfectly capturing the essence of this animal's bravery and undying loyalty.

A Dog's Tale
The Story of Hachiko

Even in peacetime there are numerous accounts of a dog's loyalty toward its owner. One tale that caught the heart of a nation was that of Hachiko, an akita who accompanied his owner back and forth to his local train station near Tokyo, in Japan. One day in May 1925 his owner died at work, so Hachiko left the station alone that evening—but he continued to return to the station every day for the rest of his life in the hope of being able to greet his master. When Hachiko himself died nine years later, a statue was erected in his memory.

Folklore generally portrays wolves as being essentially evil, whereas they are really quite shy animals by nature, rarely attacking people.

ancestor, the gray wolf, is portrayed as dangerous and sly. The difference in perception is illustrated in the Welsh story of Gelert.

In the early 1200s Llewelyn the Great owned Gelert, a hound with whom he had established a close bond of trust. One day Llewelyn set out hunting alone, leaving Gelert to guard his infant son, but when he returned home, he was horrified to see blood around Gelert's jaws. Fearing the worst, he immediately killed the hound by plunging a sword through his heart. As Llewelyn collapsed,

overcome with grief, he spotted the body of a dead wolf lying under the table—Gelert had bravely killed the wolf, defending Llewelyn's son, who was playing quite uninjured in the room next door. (Tales of this type may be only partially true, of course, but they reflect the changing way in which dogs, particularly hounds, were being viewed. No longer were they regarded as animals; instead, they were being accorded the same virtues of trust and fidelity that were central to the aristocratic code of chivalry during this era.)

The Legend of the Black Dog

One of the most consistent features of British folklore is its accounts of black dogs. These not only date back many centuries but are often linked to traditional routes across the landscape in place names such as Black Dog Lane. Folklore historians who have studied this phenomenon have linked the incidence of black dog sightings back to ancient areas of human settlement; they are often common in specific areas, such as burial grounds, and at crossroads, which were once sites for execution.

In some cases black dogs are benign companions helping to protect travelers—particularly women walking on their own. What is interesting about such accounts is that often the dog appears only at a certain spot and reappears here again when the person is walking back. Mapping

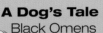

A Dog's Tale
Black Omens

In some cases there have been links reported between the appearance of a black dog and a death. However, it is not only a black dog that is a harbinger of death—there was once a widespread belief that a dog howling at night outside the home of a sick person indicated that the patient would soon die, especially if the dog came back again after being chased away.

the appearance and disappearance points suggests that sightings are most common along pasture, or ley, lines. It has been suggested that some form of energy may flow along these paths in the same way that an electrical current is transmitted through wires.

The Ley Line Mystery

This concept of ley lines as energy routes through the landscape has gained greater credence over recent

Mysterious black dogs are very commonly portrayed as a symbol of evil—as seen in this illustration from *Faust* by Goethe, the story of a medieval scholar who makes a pact with the devil.

Opposite: A loyal Newfoundland dog waits for his master to return. With their acute hearing and recognition of our individual footfalls, dogs can detect our approach from some distance away.

years, thanks to feng-shui, a Chinese discipline that recognizes the Earth's hidden energies and draws on it to change the environment. Exactly how these ley lines could result in the emergence of the shape of a black dog has not yet been explained.

Around the World

Accounts of black dogs are not confined to the British Isles; there are numerous tales from various parts of the world, including North America. A black dog called Snarly Yow is a well-known example seen in the vicinity of South Mountain, which lies just to the east of Hagerstown, Maryland. There have been literally

Below: An illustration from *The Hound of the Baskervilles*, by Sir Arthur Conan Doyle, when Sherlock Holmes and his companion, Dr. Watson, encounter an apparent canine ghost.

Dognosis
Sixth Sense?

A report on a wartime messenger dog illustrates the amazing ability of our canine companions to find their way in unknown territory. The dog, Sandy, was with advancing American troops pinned down by Japanese fire and was sent with a message requesting help from Battalion Command. Although Sandy had not seen the rest of his unit since the night before and they were now in a new location, he unerringly found his way to the correct foxhole through tall grass, across a river, beneath a curtain of mortar and tank fire and over a barbed wire fence.

hundreds of sightings over the course of the past century, and Snarly Yow often appears on the National Pike, now known as Alternate Route 40. Witnesses describe him as being jet-black, with ferocious teeth and a general air of menace, but despite appearing aggressive, there are no accounts of him attacking anyone.

Even in recent years there have been a number of trusted eyewitness accounts of close encounters with Snarly Yow. A common feature of many of these stories is that horses, in particular, seem terrified of the apparition, sometimes rearing up and throwing their rider. A few brave people have attempted to follow the dog, only to see him simply disappear before their eyes. One huntsman who

tried to shoot the beast found that all the bullets passed right through the target, making no impression. Snarly Yow does seem to have some physical presence, however; some witnesses describe the way in which he disturbs the ground when running, and in one instance, when he was hit by a vehicle, the car occupants described a distinct thud from the impact. To this day no one knows why there are so many sightings of a black dog in this particular area.

Ghostly Dogs

There are several accounts of ghostly pet dogs appearing in various ways. These generally defy any rational explanation, although if the dog happens to appear again in his usual environment, it is possible that memories of a beloved pet may have projected a view of him in the mind's eye. The dog has been seen by his owners many thousands of times during his lifetime in that position, so even after the initial, intensely emotional, aspect of losing a beloved pet has long passed, memories are subconsciously suggesting that he is still there.

Even more unexpectedly, ghostly dogs are sometimes captured on film. There are a number of cases of phantom dogs appearing in

Opposite: A young girl being comforted by her loyal companion in Riviere's painting, *Sympathy*, 1877.

A Dog's Tale
Scent or Supernatural?

Some people believe that dogs can see ghosts because of the way they sometimes behave—and it is not very hard to see how this could happen. Imagine that you are crossing a dark, eerie piece of ground—near an old burial ground perhaps—and your dog freezes momentarily, staring intently in a particular direction. The hackles along his back rise, and he starts growling, although you see nothing there. Even during daylight this could be a scary experience.

The most likely explanation is not a supernatural one, however. Your dog has probably picked up the scent of another animal in the immediate vicinity, which is lurking out of sight. A dog's superior senses explain why police, security firms, and the military often use dogs when patrolling, especially at night.

photographs alongside their owners after their death, in an era before photographic manipulation was routine. These photographic images may be explained by a trick of the light, by some flaw in the original photographic plate or film, or by a problem in the development process.

Dogs' acute senses mean they pick up scents and tune in to frequencies undetectable by humans.

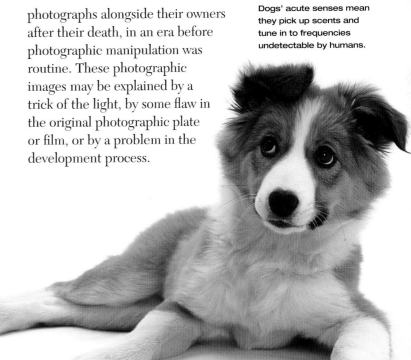

With their superior senses, dogs can be trained to help us in many ways, such as detecting explosives or aiding the disabled.

Dogs Today

A belief in the loyalty of dogs remains as strong as ever in many cultures and is reinforced still further by the changing roles that dogs fulfill today. Their ability to detect the scent of explosives, for instance, has reinforced a sense of assurance in an era when terrorism is all too real. Their willingness to please means that for some time they have been trained to be the eyes and ears of blind or deaf owners. Now, following anecdotal evidence, trials are under way to find what other health benefits dogs may be able to bring to humans.

Helping Detect Cancers and Other Illnesses

Among these trials, investigations are continuing to discover whether or not dogs are able to use their acute scenting skills to detect signs of illness in humans, specifically whether they

Is Your Dog Psychic?

There is a growing body of scientific research suggesting that dogs can develop a very close—and almost intuitive—understanding with their owners. Unfortunately, it is very difficult to carry out reliable tests to confirm that a bond of this type has been established, but you can see if your dog will respond to your thoughts.

Sit down quietly at home, with your dog in another room. Concentrate on images of your pet in your mind's eye, perhaps reinforcing them by looking at a photograph of him. Try to call your dog to you, but without making any sound; you may find that he soon comes to your side. Even if this works, it does not prove beyond doubt that you and your dog have established a psychic bond—it may simply be that your pet has woken up and is coming to find you anyway! However, it certainly confirms that there is a close rapport between you.

can detect the presence of skin cancers at an early stage.

Dogs can be trained to aid people who are susceptible to epilepsy—they can sense, up to 45 minutes prior, when a person is likely to have an epileptic fit, thereby guiding them to safety before it happens. In a similar way, dogs can forewarn diabetic patients that their blood sugar levels are declining, helping to avoid the possibility of collapse. Dogs have also been trained to help people suffering from Parkinson's disease. Such patients often suffer from coordination problems, including a condition known as "freezing," when the legs seize suddenly, causing them to stumble and fall. If the dog senses this is about to happen, he will lean against his owner, allowing the person to continue walking safely. Such dogs are also trained to help their owners up again if they do trip and fall.

For most owners, however, it is simply the unwavering affection their dog provides that is a major tonic, especially in times of stress. Dogs intuitively pick up on our mood and have the ability to lift us out of depression, aiding both our mental and physical health.

Dogs can significantly improve our quality of life in many different ways, but especially with their unwavering affection.

Dog Behavior A-Z

Inevitably, your relationship with your dog will experience some highs and lows, but it is important to try to understand why he is behaving in a particular way so that you can deal with the problem effectively. Always contact your vet for advice initially to rule out any underlying medical problem. In many cases there is no quick fix, so it may take several months of attending consultations and carrying out exercises to achieve a lasting improvement in your dog's behavior. However, if you act quickly before the problem develops into a habit, it will be easier to curb.

A

Aggression at Home

This is the most worrying and serious of canine behavioral problems, and it has a number of causes. Even the weather can play a part in making dogs short-tempered—surveys have shown that dogs are more likely to bite during stormy weather. Possessive jealousy is perhaps the most common reason for dogs to snap at their owners, so never tease a dog with his toys or he will be reluctant to allow you to take the toy at

Dognosis
Aggressive Reactions

Although the underlying reason is not clear, there have been a number of confirmed cases of Lyme disease causing a previously docile and friendly dog to undergo a sudden change in character, becoming short-tempered and aggressive. Once the infection is treated, the dog's behavior returns to normal.

If your dog's nature suddenly changes and he also appears to be ill, a test for Lyme disease is recommended.

other times. The same applies with food—if your dog does not sit before you place his food bowl on the floor, do not take it away from him. Instead, position him in a sitting posture so he learns what is required, then put the food down without delay.

It is especially important to teach children not to tease a dog with food, because dogs perceive children as lower in the pack rank than adults and are more likely to challenge a child. If you know your dog is nervous, make sure your children are careful when playing with him— he may bite if he is frightened or if he is hurt. Biting or snapping is especially likely if your pet cannot escape or feels closed in—perhaps because the child is holding his collar. Supervision is particularly important when your children have friends visiting, because they may not have dogs themselves and have little or no understanding of how to interact with them. (See page 154.)

Aggression Toward Other Dogs

There are certain dogs that do not get along well with their own kind. For instance, the Staffordshire bull terrier was kept originally for fighting, so he may not agree well with other dogs—especially of his own breed. Male dogs in particular are especially aggressive in such cases,

and neutering is strongly recommended because this will reduce the level of the male hormone testosterone, thus making the dog much less aggressive.

Aggression Toward People

When out for a walk in a park, children may rush up to pet your dog without any prior warning, and this may provoke an aggressive response, partly due to your dog's instinct to protect you. If you leave your dog in a car on his own, passersby will sometimes taunt him, causing your pet to start leaping back and forth over the seats, barking and snarling—particularly if the person concerned is banging on the car windows and encouraging him. This situation is especially dangerous if the window has been left partially open, because your dog may be able to bite through the gap.

Dogs who mix readily with people of all ages from puppyhood are most likely to grow up into well-adjusted adults. However, the ancestry of the breed does play a part—the rottweiler, for instance, was originally created as a guardian, so the breed tends to be more suspicious of strangers than breeds kept simply for companionship.

Aggression (Uncontrolled)

Cases of dogs suddenly becoming completely uncontrollable are rare, although a familial link to this type of behavior has been identified in certain bloodlines of the cocker spaniel.

Rabies, the dreaded viral infection, affects the brain and will cause a previously well-adjusted dog to become uncontrollably aggressive in the latter stages of illness. In areas where rabies is endemic, dogs must always be immunized against this disease, whether or not this is required by law.

Appetite Loss

Dogs generally eat their food readily, but some—particularly smaller dogs—may be fussy and learn to be manipulative. If you offer your pet dry food

but replace it almost immediately with wet food if he shows little interest, you will soon find that he loses interest in dry food completely because he knows wet food will soon be forthcoming. Cold food straight from the refrigerator can be disconcerting, but pouring special canine gravy over it can help to rekindle a jaded appetite.

However, other factors may influence your dog's appetite. If he is nervous, he will prefer eating in a quiet area of the home; noisy events such as fireworks and thunderstorms may cause him to lose his appetite. On the other hand, your pet might have a dental problem, making eating painful, or he could be ill. An older dog with kidney failure will tend to eat less because this illness depresses the appetite. If your dog persists in refusing food, seek veterinary advice since this can often be a sign of illness—especially if your pet normally has a healthy appetite.

Attention (Seeking)

Dogs are very much creatures of habit. Although puppies can be unpredictable, waking up and displaying sudden bursts of energy, they generally settle into a routine that is influenced by your lifestyle. It is important to provide them with stability by keeping to set times for meals and walks if possible, because this will prevent your dog from becoming anxious and constantly seeking to attract attention, fearful that you may have forgotten these two central daily aspects of canine life. This is not to say that dogs are inflexible in their mindset—the opportunity for a second walk in a day is likely to be taken up just as enthusiastically as the first, as will the opportunity to eat again!

See also Whining.

B

Barking (Nighttime)

Older dogs sometimes start barking unexpectedly in the middle of the night for no obvious reason. They can even become so upset that they spoil their surroundings. The condition is generally

called Canine Alzheimer's disease, since it reflects a state of mental confusion. There is no long-term cure for this condition, but there are drugs available to alleviate it, so seek veterinary advice. Some prescription diets are specially formulated with ingredients that may help to maintain an older dog's mental health.

Biting

There is a very distinct difference between an inadvertent nip during a game and a deliberate bite. Any dog who bites is definitely a distinct liability, so you will need to seek advice from your vet regarding your pet's future. This is not a situation that you can resolve on your own—you must seek professional advice.

Burying Bones

Some dogs—such as terriers, who dig instinctively—frequently bury bones in the garden. This can be maddening for avid gardeners, since the dog will often choose to dig a hole in the soft soil of flower beds, thus scattering the plants. Dogs bury bones

so they can return to feed on them at a later date, in a similar way to wild dogs concealing excess food from scavengers. Covering the bones with soil also prevents flies from laying eggs on them. The resulting maggots would eat the meat and might make it unhealthy for the dog.

Dogs may also attempt to conceal surplus food by pushing their food bowl out of sight, sometimes pawing at it to move it to a less accessible part of the room, since it is not really feasible to bury small pieces of dry food or to carry wet food from a can or pouch outdoors. Bones, on the other hand, are easily moved in the mouth and can be an ongoing source of food, which is why they are favored for burying.

Toys may also sometimes be buried, especially if they are impregnated with a slight scent of food. While he digs the hole, a dog will keep hold of the item with his front legs. He then simply drops it into the hole and usually covers it using his nose. Thus, you can often tell when your dog has been digging, because his nose will be dusty with soil. *See also* Digging.

C

Chasing Joggers and Bicyclists

Dogs are playful by nature, and a young puppy will often bound along after someone who is jogging, usually with little harm done. However, it is more dangerous if your dog chases after someone on a bicycle, because this could lead to a serious accident—he may get caught in the spokes or, worse, get hit by a car. It is therefore important to have your dog under control so he will not behave this way when he is likely to encounter a bicyclist. A puppy will have more energy than an older dog and be more easily distracted, so try to allow your pet to watch joggers and bicyclists while on a leash so he comes to realize that they are part of the everyday scene and lose interest in chasing them.

Chewing

Dogs have an instinctive desire to chew, stemming from the way their ancestors gnawed on the bones of prey to supplement their calcium intake—meat itself has very low calcium content. While today's formulated foods contain sufficient calcium to meet your pet's needs, this instinctive behavior remains strong. Many dogs enjoy bones, but these may be messy indoors and can attract flies outside. The bones themselves should be thick and not prone to splintering—chicken bones should never be given to dogs, because they splinter easily and the sharp ends can lodge in the mouth or the throat, causing your dog to start choking. Chewing can be beneficial for dogs because it helps to keep the teeth clean and free from a buildup of tartar. There are specially designed dental chews available for this.

Young dogs are especially prone to being destructive when teething; they will chew on a

Types of Aggressive Behavior

Behaviorists categorize displays of aggressive behavior based on their cause, although there can be more than one underlying reason behind a dog's actions.

1. Food-related aggression—If a dog has been teased with food as a puppy, it may growl and snap when feeding.
2. Fearful aggression—A nervous dog that appears submissive may respond aggressively if backed into a corner.
3. Hierarchical aggression—Male dogs, in particular, may feel threatened by another dog and react aggressively.
4. Possessive aggression—Dogs may lash out in defense of toys or bones.
5. Territorial aggression—Dogs teased while in confined spaces, such as cars, may try to bite.
6. Protective aggression—A dog may show aggression toward people if he thinks his owner is being attacked.
7. Drug-related aggression—Some medicines have side effects that result in aggressive behavior.
8. Sickness-related aggression—The least common cause, but feeling unwell can make your dog exhibit a poor temper.

In most cases of aggression, a dog will give a series of coded warnings. The most noticeable of these are curling his lips, exposing his canine teeth as a warning gesture, and growling more loudly. His hackles will also probably be raised.

wide variety of household objects, from table and chair legs through to mobile phones and remote-control units for televisions and other electrical equipment. Shoes are often a particular favorite! The simplest solution is to be aware and not leave tempting items within reach. Provide a range of suitable toys for your dog to chew to ease the irritation from his new teeth erupting. Damage is especially likely if you shut a young dog in a room and leave him on his own for any length of time, so always try to keep your pet with you when he is teething. It is probably not worth buying him a permanent bed until after this phase has passed, because it may get badly damaged or destroyed.

Once the teething phase has passed, a dog's desire to chew is usually greatly reduced—although many dogs enjoy gnawing on an old stick when out for a walk. It is not a good idea to throw a stick for your dog, because you might hit him if he jumps up at the wrong moment, so only use soft toys when playing with your pet.

A dog is also more likely to be destructive if he is bored. If you need to go out and cannot take him with you, encourage him to exercise well by playing with him in the backyard or taking him out for a walk beforehand so he is more likely to sleep in your absence. There is little point in scolding him if you come home and find he has caused damage, because he will not be able to understand what he has done wrong if he has not been caught in the act. If you are concerned about your puppy, the best solution is a large crate with space for a water bowl and a bed, where the puppy can be housed temporarily while you are out.

Crying
This problem begins in puppyhood, because a young dog whimpers to attract his mother's attention, but it may develop into a habit if the puppy realizes that it is guaranteed to attract your attention. Puppies often whimper when they want food or if they are shut out, so the solution is not to allow your pet to get into a situation where he needs to cry regularly, so that it becomes a habit.

Allow your puppy to move around freely and stick to regular mealtimes—following a clear routine from the outset will avoid many potential behavioral problems in the future. The situation is different if you have taken on an older dog. Crying in this case can often be a symptom of separation anxiety (see page 174), which will also need to be addressed.

D

Destructive Behavior

It is normal for dogs to scratch at a cushion or the fabric of their bed before settling down to sleep as a way of making themselves comfortable. There is little that can be done about this, apart from covering, or keeping your dog away from, expensive furnishings, especially leather chairs.

Dogs also tend to scratch at doors. Your pet will quickly learn to find his way from room to room by pressing against a door with his nose or paw, or a combination of both. The problem arises on the other side of the door when he wants to return—he will use his paws to try to open the door, and when he is unable to do so, he will try standing against it, balancing on hind legs with his claws dragging down the paintwork or glass. Over time this may not only damage the surface paintwork but also create divets in the wood.

Fitting a curtain over it may protect the door, but you could also leave it ajar so your dog can move around freely in rooms where he is allowed regular access. Dogs such as beagles, which have a relatively compact body shape, are more likely to behave in this way than greyhounds, for example, with their long bodies.

The back door is likely to be damaged if your dog tries to get back indoors after being out in the backyard. You may not want to leave this door open, so anticipate your dog's movements: If he is outside, don't just wait for him to come back and start scratching at the door—take the initiative and call him back inside so he will not need to scratch or bark to be let in again, which can also develop rapidly into a habit.
See also Chewing.

Digging

Certain dogs are instinctively more inclined to dig than others. Terriers, in particular, are likely to excavate flower beds, scattering precious bulbs or plants, or dig random holes in a lawn, because they were bred to hunt vermin such as rats, which sometimes entailed digging their way

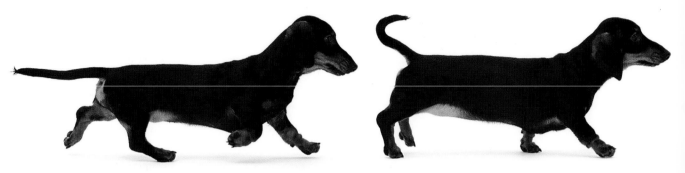

underground or moving rocks to reach their quarry. However, before blaming your dog for such damage, bear in mind that local wildlife may have been responsible. Dogs also dig holes to bury bones or toys.

Chemical deterrents from a pet store or garden outlet can often dissuade a dog from digging up a specific area of the garden, but although they can be effective, such treatments usually need to be reapplied again after it has rained. An alternative solution is to use netting to exclude your dog and protect the area if it is not too large. Generally, however, dogs do prefer to play on open areas of lawn rather than venturing into the flower beds—unless there is something in them that has attracted their attention.

Disturbing Behavior

Effective treatment for behavioral problems requires an individual assessment of your pet, and you will probably have to describe the history of the problem in detail. It may be helpful to consult other members of the family and then jot down some notes before you go to visit the behaviorist because you will then be less likely to forget something that you later wish you had mentioned. In a few cases drug therapy may help, but this tends to alleviate only the worst symptoms and rarely solves a behavioral problem.

Dragging Hindquarters

This behavior, known as scooting, may look quite alarming because it appears as if your dog has suddenly lost the strength in his hind legs or suffered a temporary form of paralysis. In reality, the cause is a blockage of the pair of anal sacs (sometimes called glands), which lie just inside the rectum. These sacs are about the size of a pea, and when they are blocked, it is very uncomfortable for your dog, so he will drag his hindquarters along the ground to try to relieve the irritation.

The solution is for your vet to empty these sacs by squeezing them to remove the foul-smelling liquid, but it is not uncommon for the problem to recur. Adding some bran—as sold in pet stores for guinea pigs and horses—to your dog's food may help to prevent a recurrence. Mix

the bran with a little water and add it to dry food, or simply stir it into wet food. If this fails to alleviate the problem, it may be necessary for your vet to anesthetize your dog and wash out the sacs with saline solution, then give antibiotics to reduce the risk of infection. If the problem is left untreated, your dog is likely to become constipated because it will be painful for him to relieve himself, and it is also likely that infection will break through to the skin around the anus, creating anal fistulae, which can be difficult to treat.

Dreaming

Before settling down to sleep, a dog will circle around his chosen spot, which mimics the way a wolf might trample down vegetation before lying down on the ground. When a dog first falls asleep, he will often curl up into a ball—particularly if he is small—because this helps him to stay warm by trapping his body heat. However, before long your dog will probably roll onto his side and you may notice that his legs start twitching as if he is running, and his whiskers may also twitch. This

Dognosis
How Much Exercise?

Dogs vary significantly in the level of exercise they require, but their needs can be ascertained by looking into the background of the breed in question. Scent hounds, herding dogs, and gundogs rank among the most active and display great stamina. In contrast, some dogs are not well suited to an energetic lifestyle, such as many toy breeds and some larger dogs, such as the bulldog. You need to be sensitive to the amount of exercise that your dog requires—do not assume that giant breeds, such as the Irish wolfhound or great Dane, will benefit from long walks at an early age; overexertion when young can lead to joint problems later in life.

Regular, smaller amounts of daily exercise will be much better for both of you than one marathon hike over the weekend. If you are feeling tired from your exertions, your dog probably will be as well—especially because he is likely to have covered more ground than you have, running back and forth exploring while you have been walking in a straight line.

is a sign that he is in deep or "rapid eyeball movement" (REM) sleep; his eyelids will also be moving, although this may be less apparent.

During periods of REM sleep—which are usually quite brief—your pet is less likely to respond to you, although generally most dogs are quite light sleepers. This makes them invaluable as guardians, even though they may spend over half the day asleep or dozing. The old saying "Let sleeping dogs lie" has a basis in fact, because once a dog has woken up, he will not be inclined to go back to sleep again immediately.

Ear Scratching

The ear shape in dogs varies widely, and some dogs are at greater risk of ear infections than others. The heavy, trailing ears of spaniels, such as the American cocker spaniel, predispose them to infections because the ear canal is sealed off, creating ideal conditions for fungi and bacteria to multiply. The intense irritation that results will cause your dog to scratch almost constantly at one or both ears, depending on the extent of the problem. In some cases ear mites may also be present, although this is less likely if you have used a long-acting flea treatment, since these also offer protection against ear mites.

Your pet may injure himself if he continues scratching an ear, because the earflap may start bleeding internally, creating a hematoma. This is not painful, but it will make the ear look unsightly. If the infection can be treated, the dog will stop persistently scratching and the swelling should disperse, although there is a risk that some distortion will remain. In the most serious cases surgery may be required to assist the healing process.

Never be tempted to poke anything down your dog's ears, especially if he has an infection, because it will probably be intensely painful for him and may cause him to snap at you. If applying eardrops, allow them to run down the ear canal as instructed, then gently massage the base of the ear to help disperse the medication. Keep to the recommended treatment schedule and do not stop using the medication early, even if you think your dog has recovered; there is a real risk that the infection may reemerge and be significantly harder to treat if the microbes have become resistant to the treatment.

Eating Habits (Messy)

If you include large pieces of cooked meat in your dog's diet, he may drag a lump of it out of his food bowl onto the floor because he needs to use his carnassial teeth to slice through it and chew it into pieces small enough to swallow. He will eat with his head tilted to one side, the meat will be on the floor, and it can all be quite messy. To resolve this, cut the meat up into small pieces. With dry food your pet will be able to pick the kibbles up with the incisor teeth at the front of the mouth, swallowing them down whole without chewing them. If your dog is naturally a messy eater, place his food bowl on a special mat that can easily be wiped after he has eaten. Keep his food bowl and the surrounding area clean or flies may be attracted here, especially in hot weather.

Excessive Barking

One of the major reasons for complaints about dogs in urban areas is persistent barking that upsets the neighbors. Some breeds, such as Chihuahuas, are naturally noisier than others, while greyhounds rank among the quietest. You may want your pet to alert you to the approach of a stranger, but not to bark all the time. Dogs may also bark when they meet each other while out for a walk and when traveling in a vehicle. Sometimes spraying a dog with a water pistol may dissuade him from barking repeatedly.

Exercise

For most people, there are a limited number of options for walking their dog near where they live. However, a daily walk is important for dogs, not just for physical exercise—especially if it provides an opportunity to run off the leash—but also for mental stimulation. Do not worry that your pet will be bored by visiting the same locality every day—after all, this is not dissimilar to the way in which wolves move regularly around their territory. There will be new scents to investigate each time, and probably different dogs around as well, so to your dog every excursion will be different.

F

Fever

The danger from ticks is not that they feed on a dog's blood, but that they can transmit serious illnesses. In many parts of the world—including North America and the United Kingdom—ticks are a major vector of Lyme disease, also known as borreliosis after the bacterium that causes this illness. Signs of an infection can be variable—they may include both fever and joint pain, resulting in lameness. In a more serious form of the disease, the kidneys may be affected, and this is often fatal in dogs. Treatment with antibiotics can be successful, especially where the infection primarily affects the joints, but it is not always easy to eliminate the bacteria completely. As a protective measure, keep your dog away from areas where ticks are prevalent—particularly

Dognosis
Paw Prints

It is not just the length of the coat and its relative thickness that influences a dog's ability to control his body temperature. Unlike humans, dogs cannot sweat effectively—the only corresponding type of sweat glands they have are located between the paws. During hot weather you may see paw prints when your dog walks across a cold tiled floor, formed from droplets of sweat—although these will be far less conspicuous than if his feet were muddy, and they disappear as soon as the moisture evaporates.

during spring and fall, when the numbers of ticks seeking hosts will be at their highest. It may be possible to have your dog immunized against borreliosis; if so, the injection should be given early in life, from nine weeks of age onward, depending on the type of vaccine used.

If you find ticks on your dog's skin, your instinctive reaction may be to pull them out, but this is likely to leave the mouthparts anchored in the skin, which could easily trigger an infection—or infective microbes in the tick's body may be spread to your dog. Never squeeze a tick's body, because this may put you at risk from a tick-borne infection, especially if you have any cuts on your fingers. Instead, you need to persuade the parasite to loosen its grip. There are special sprays and tools available for this, but the simplest solution is

to cover the tick's body with petroleum jelly, paying particular attention to its rear end. This blocks the tick's breathing tube, causing it to release its grip. Providing the tick drops off within a day of attaching, the risk of any disease being spread to your dog is minimal.

If you have treated your dog with a spot-on treatment to kill fleas, it should work in the same way and just as effectively against ticks. In areas where these parasites are prevalent, ensure that your pet is consistently protected—although it is best to vary the type of treatment at intervals to reduce the likelihood of ticks acquiring resistance to the active ingredients. Specially impregnated collars to deter ticks are not a good idea if you have more than one dog, because they may pull the collars off each other and swallow the toxic chemicals. The effective range of the collar also tends to be limited, because the tick needs to come into contact with the chemicals so the collar will only protect the area around itself. *See also* Lethargy, Parasites, Red Urine, Symptoms of Sickness.

Fighting

If you meet an aggressive dog when you are out for a walk, call your pet back to you. If fighting breaks out, do not try to place your hand or arms between the dogs to separate them, because this will almost inevitably lead to you being bitten. You may have to drag your dog away by grabbing his collar from behind the neck; if you have a walking stick, you can drive off the other dog, which should lose interest as you and your pet retreat.

If your dog is the aggressor, hold on to his collar and twist it as you pull him away, which will cause him to choke momentarily. Lifting his front legs off the ground at the same time should also help to prevent him from behaving aggressively.

G

Grass (Eating)

Some dogs regularly eat grass, usually when they are out on a walk, and they may also seek out various weeds, often being specific in their choice. These plants serve as a dietary supplement, reflecting the dog's omnivorous feeding habits. Eating grass can also sometimes serve as a means to induce vomiting if your dog is feeling off color. The most common cause in such cases is the presence of intestinal parasites, so if your dog has not been dewormed recently, then try this to overcome the problem.

See also Symptoms of Sickness.

H

Hair Loss

Loss of hair, particularly in breeds such as dachshunds, should always be investigated by your vet without delay because it can be indicative of a potentially serious parasitic disease caused by *Demodex* mites.

Heat Stroke

The primary way that dogs cool themselves is via their nasal cavities; the blood flow here releases heat, which triggers the evaporation of fluid from the nose. Breeds with short, rounded faces, such as boxers and pugs, are at risk of suffering from heat stroke because their nasal cavities are so short that they find it more difficult to stay cool. Avoid exercising dogs of this type when the weather is hot, because they might collapse from heat stroke. Be very wary if

Feeding Time

Owners sometimes worry that if they offer their pet the same food every day, he will become bored. There is no evidence to support this, but most manufacturers have different flavors, so it is easy to introduce some variety to your pet's diet. Be wary of suddenly altering the type of food, however—switching from wet to dry food, for example—since this is likely to result in digestive upsets. Some dogs can become very particular about what food they will eat. Small dogs especially can be rather fussy about food and may not appreciate a change in diet.

your pet starts panting heavily—this is a warning sign, especially if he is suffering from an underlying heart ailment. Move him to a cool location, where he can rest and recover, with water available. Always take a bowl and drinking water when you are out together for a walk in hot weather.
See also Lethargy, Panting.

Hunting

Many dogs have retained their hunting instincts. Although retired greyhounds make wonderful companions, they should be kept muzzled in public places if they are let off the leash, because they may instinctively chase after smaller dogs that they can easily catch and injure. Scent hounds are more likely to set off after a scent and disappear into the distance, ignoring your calls to return. This is especially likely in rural areas, where they may pick up the scent of rabbits. The hunting strategies of terriers are different; they are avid killers of rodents, making them popular on farms, but if you are out for a walk near rabbit warrens, your pet may suddenly vanish underground. This may not matter, but occasionally terriers do get

stuck underground, and it can be very difficult to track down your pet if you are not sure exactly where he disappeared. There are special collars available that enable you to monitor the position of your pet at all times when out walking, and these can be very useful in this situation. Always be wary about exercising a terrier in this type of terrain, though—especially if you are on vacation—because it will cause a great deal of worry and perhaps a serious problem if he does disappear. Be very careful in the vicinity of cliffs as well, because terriers often show no fear of heights and may disappear over the edge.

I

Illness

Provided you keep your dog's immunizations up to date, there should be little to worry about in terms of serious illness, unless your pet is afflicted by a genetic problem. Dogs do suffer from an upset stomach on occasion—largely as a result of their scavenging habits, which can lead to vomiting, diarrhea, or both. If this is mild, simply starve your dog for a day, making sure he has free access to drinking water. Reintroduce food with a bland diet such as chicken and rice for a few days afterward.

If a young dog is affected or there are signs of blood in the bowels, then seek veterinary advice immediately. Any change in your dog's behavior, such as apparent constipation, will also need investigating by your vet. In a young dog there may be an obstruction in the intestinal tract caused by something he has eaten, which will need urgent treatment.
See also Dragging Hindquarters, Grass (Eating), Lethargy, Symptoms of Sickness.

J

Joint Pain
See Fever, Lethargy, Parasites.

Jumping Up
Many dogs instinctively jump up, particularly when they are excited, just because they want to get closer to your face. Even a small dog or puppy jumping up exuberantly could hurt someone with his claws, while a large dog behaving in this way may knock a person over, so it is important to dissuade your dog from behaving this way. Say, "Down," lifting his paws down to the ground if necessary, and put your outstretched palm out to emphasize the instruction. Then walk away and ignore your dog for a short time. Jumping up is often about seeking attention, so always remember to bend down and stroke your pet as a greeting when you come home, since this should remove the need for him to jump up.

Fleas in the Home

An IGR treatment will not protect your dog from acquiring fleas, but their value is clear once you realize just how prolific fleas can be. A single female is able to lay literally thousands of eggs, which will be deposited in the dog's immediate environment—mostly in the area where he sleeps. When treating an infestation, it is therefore vital to wash all your pet's bedding, as well as the bed, and to vacuum thoroughly to remove any flea eggs and tiny larvae, which tend to congregate along the edge of baseboards. Otherwise, you could face a major flea epidemic and you will have to call in a pest-control company to treat the room—or even your entire home—to eliminate these parasites.

L

Lethargy

If your dog is lethargic, he may be tired or it may be due to hot weather, but he may also be suffering from an infection. Ehrlichiosis is a tick-borne illness to which dogs are susceptible, often spread by the brown dog tick and common throughout North America. It is caused by a group of microbes known as *Ehrlichia*, which have the characteristics of both bacteria and viruses. *Ehrlichia* multiply in the body, often causing enlargement of the spleen, liver, and the lymph nodes. Infective organisms are found in the blood only early in the course of the infection, so your vet may have to carry out several tests to confirm ehrlichiosis. As well as being lethargic, your dog may have little appetite, be short of breath, or suffer from joint pain. There is a more chronic form of the illness, which does not show for at least a month after the initial bite. This can result in a range of different symptoms, including swelling in the hind legs, eye inflammation, and weight loss. The situation can be worse if the tick is carrying both babesiosis and ehrlichiosis because it can transmit both with a single bite.

See also Heat Stroke, Panting, Parasites, Red Urine, Symptoms of Sickness.

Licking

Puppies seek solid food from their mother by licking at the sides of her lips to encourage her to regurgitate food for them. As they grow older, licking retains a social dimension within a pack setting; a subordinate dog may lick another of higher social standing in the group as a form of grooming. Dogs may also sometimes lick their owners in this way, too.

A dog may sometimes groom himself by licking or nibbling at his coat. This can help to cool the body in hot weather and also helps to remove dirt, especially mud, from the coat. It may also be a way of relieving irritation or aiding the healing of minor wounds—canine saliva is

slightly acidic, so it can help to prevent the development of microbes that might otherwise cause an infection.

M

Mating

When mating, a male dog climbs up onto the female and uses his forelegs to help him maintain his balance and hold on to her, supporting his weight on his hind legs. Unfortunately, a young male dog will sometimes behave in a similar fashion when you are sitting down. He may suddenly decide to grab the top of one of your legs with his front paws, which can be embarrassing, especially if you have guests. Push him down immediately to discourage him, although the only long-term solution is to have him neutered. In the short term you can try the homeopathic remedy gelsemium, which may lower his overall sex drive.

Creating a Safer Environment

Ticks tend to thrive in areas of brush with some trees and open areas of grass. However, the brown dog tick (*Rhipicephalus sanguineus*) is common in more suburban areas—especially where there are untidy backyards. It is capable of spreading a number of infections to dogs, so make every effort to keep this parasite away from your home. Keep the grass cut short, sweep up old leaves, and remove dead plants from flower borders to deter them from colonizing the area. Occasionally, ticks may even invade the home— and they can represent a real threat to the health of your family. Choose an insecticidal powder that is safe for your pets, and use it around the floor area to prevent any ticks from climbing up the interior walls.

Gelsemium is generally available from stores that sell herbal remedies.

N

Nervousness

Dogs can be nervous of people, other dogs, traveling in cars, or loud noises such as fireworks. Signs of nervousness will be clear from your pet's body language—he will be cowering and may even start growling or attempt to bite in extreme circumstances. The root cause of this is likely to be either a lack of socialization early in life or subsequent mistreatment. It is important to identify the cause correctly to find a solution. Herbal remedies, such as skullcap or valerian tablets, may help in some cases.

You may need sedatives from your vet if traveling is upsetting for your dog and you have to take him on a trip with you. In this case try taking short trips for pleasurable experiences, such as walks, which may help to overcome your dog's fear.

Nibbling at Skin

If a flea infestation is left untreated, there is an increased risk that your dog will develop a fleabite allergy, which will cause him a great deal of discomfort. The allergic reaction is to the flea's saliva, and every time your dog is bitten in the future, it will be intensely irritating, leading him to nibble ferociously at his skin in an attempt to relieve the problem.

Certain breeds are especially vulnerable to this type of reaction—notably dobermans, which tend to be sensitive to other skin conditions as well. You will need anti-allergy tablets from your vet to treat a fleabite allergy.
See also Parasites, Scratching (Himself).

P

Panting

Not all dogs like hot weather, so if your pet is panting heavily, try to keep him as cool as possible. If you do not have air-conditioning, a portable fan in the area where your dog spends much of his time will help air to circulate when the weather is hot. Your pet may also want to lie on a stone or tiled floor—often changing his sleeping habits quite dramatically in an attempt to stay cool. Always be careful that there is fresh drinking water constantly available so your pet will not become dehydrated. If your dog has a heart ailment, dehydration can lead to serious illness. *See also* Heat Stroke, Lethargy.

Parasites

The brown dog tick can be a serious menace to your dog's health if he swallows it, because the tick may itself be infected by the protozoal parasite *Hepatozoon canis*. This infection, which is more likely to be encountered in Gulf Coast states than anywhere else, results in an initial fever, which is followed by lameness, muscle pain, and weakness. The parasites settle in a group of white blood cells called neutrophils. This infection emphasizes the need to be alert for signs of ticks on your pet, because there is currently no effective treatment.

Fleas are also able to pass on parasites, such as tapeworms, to a dog—the flea carries the immature tapeworm in its body, so if the dog swallows it, the tapeworm will complete its lifecycle in the dog's intestinal tract. You should therefore dose your dog for tapeworms if he has recently suffered from fleas.

See also Ear Scratching, Fever, Lethargy, Nibbling at Skin, Scratching (Himself), Red Urine.

R

Red Urine

Ticks spread a number of other illnesses. Babesiosis is caused by a microscopic blood parasite, similar to an amoeba, and is often described as "red water" because the parasites invade red blood cells and break them down, causing the dog's urine to turn red. Other signs are likely to include fever, while the kidneys and other body organs may also be damaged. Even with prompt treatment the chances of recovery are not good and blood transfusions may be required. Dogs that do recover may remain carriers for some time, passing the infection on to any ticks that bite them.

See also Fever, Lethargy, Parasites.

Reluctance to Move

Sometimes your dog may seem reluctant to move, dragging behind or even sitting down when you try to coax him along on the leash. This is often a sign of fear—it often occurs on a visit to the vet, particularly if your dog has bad memories of a previous trip there.

If you have a small dog, the simplest way of dealing with this problem is to pick up your pet and carry him into the vet's premises. With a larger dog this may not be possible, and it is certainly not a good idea to pull him along on the leash, because you may injure his neck. Try heading off in the opposite direction, which should encourage your dog to stand and start walking again, then cross the road repeatedly, coming back down the other side. This change of direction may be sufficient to disorientate him so that you arrive at the vet's door before he realizes where he is. An alternative solution is to tie him up securely while you go and ask for assistance at the vet's offices.

Dogs behaving in this way are not normally aggressive, although they may be wary with a stranger because an unfamiliar person touching them will add to their feeling of nervousness.

A similar reluctance to walk along normally may occur when you are alongside a busy road, because your dog is upset by the noise of traffic passing close by. Puppies often react in this way when you first take them out for a walk along busy streets in your neighborhood. However, becoming accustomed to busy roads is an important aspect of learning about the world around them, so the best solution is to pause to allow your dog to see what is upsetting him. Once he realizes that he is not in danger, he should walk on normally with some encouragement, and before long he will come to ignore passing traffic.

If you have taken on an older dog, perhaps from an animal welfare shelter, you may find he has some irrational fears. These are almost certainly the result of bad past experiences and they may not immediately be apparent when you acquire the dog. It might be a particular style of clothing that is the problem, due to a resemblance to the clothing of someone who mistreated him in the past. These problems may be hard to

overcome, so you will need to be sensitive and try to avoid exposing your pet to what upsets him, if at all possible.

Another possible cause of nervousness and reluctance to move forward is if another dog has attacked your dog recently while you were out on a walk. This can make him reluctant to follow the same route again—at least in the short term. Try varying your walk for a few weeks to reduce any lingering fears in your pet's mind—and perhaps go at a different time of day. This should also reduce the likelihood that you will meet the other dog again.

Rolling Around

Dogs are most likely to roll around on a warm surface in order to stretch and remain supple. A dog may also roll over onto his back to seek affection from people whom he knows well. Far less desirably, it can be a way to pick up scents from the ground to reinforce his own—this usually means finding an unpleasant, strong-smelling deposit to roll in, such as cow dung or fox excrement.

S

Scooting
See Dragging Hindquarters.

Scratching (Himself)
If your dog is scratching more than usual and perhaps nibbling intently at his skin, the problem is likely to be an infestation of fleas. The fleas use their mouthparts to inject saliva into the dog's skin when they feed, so the bites are very irritating. Although you may sometimes disturb an unwary flea with a conventional comb, the fine teeth of a flea comb mean there is little likelihood of a flea being able to slip through and remain undetected.

When you groom your pet for fleas, take him outside so that if any fleas jump off, they are less likely to reinfest your dog than if they leap off in the home. Have a container of water ready for holding fleas you catch. The most likely area to find them is around the base of the tail, because they often congregate there rather than on the thinner fur on the underside of the body. If your dog has many fleas, the most effective way of dealing with the problem is to give him a bath with a medicated shampoo to kill them—

Keeping Him Warm

If your dog is affected by the cold, he will appreciate a warm and cozy coat to wear outside in bad weather. Dog coats are often sold by breed name, but if you have a lurcher or a similar crossbreed that is not a standard size, it is easy to measure your dog so you can buy a coat that will fit.

Measure your pet in a straight line from the base of the neck down to the root of the tail. A hook-and-loop tape closure is the best option to fasten the coat around him, because it will only be pulled open if he heads into undergrowth—unlike a button, which may be pulled off and lost.

remembering also to wash his bedding and vacuum carefully to prevent reinfestation.

Despite all your efforts, your dog may easily acquire fleas during his daily travels just by

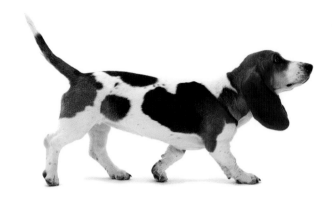

meeting another animal that has them. You will need to be alert, particularly during the warmer summer months—although in modern centrally heated homes fleas can be a problem at any time of the year. Even a young puppy can suffer from fleas, which may have been brought into the home by the family cat. An anti-flea spray is a good second line of defense against occasional fleas, but if using more than one product, make sure they are compatible.

When treating your dog with a long-acting preparation, always note the treatment date in a diary so you can be certain when the next treatment is due. Although dogs and cats do, in theory, have different types of flea, they can cross-infect each other. If your dog has fleas, you must treat your cat, too, to prevent the dog from becoming reinfected. However, you will need to use a different treatment because many flea preparations that are intended for dogs are actually harmful to cats. You will also need to take particular care in the choice of preparation when treating puppies.

If your dog does get fleas, you may be bitten yourself, which will lead to a very irritating reddish circular area on the skin—often around the ankles where the flea has jumped up from the floor. But, luckily, neither dog nor cat fleas can live on humans for any length of time. *See also* Nibbling at Skin.

Scratching (Furniture)
See Destructive Behavior.

Separation Anxiety
This is a surprisingly common problem in dogs. Being social by nature and used to being part of a family, your dog may feel uneasy and worried about being left alone. He may start barking loudly—and you may become aware of the problem only after a neighbor mentions that your dog barks repeatedly when you are out—or he may cause considerable damage in your home when you are not there.

The answer is first to give your dog plenty of exercise so he sleeps well in your absence, but

also try to vary the length of time that you are away so you are not following a set routine that your dog can learn. Go out for just a few minutes; then on another occasion go shopping for an hour or more. Although this may seem strange, the fact that the length of your absence is unpredictable means that your dog should be less disturbed. Finally, leave him with a range of toys to play with—especially chews—so that he can amuse himself with them instead of chewing your belongings.

Shivering

A smaller dog is more vulnerable to the cold than a larger one, simply because the surface area of his body is relatively large compared to his volume, so it is harder to maintain his core body temperature. However, other factors—such as the coat type— are also quite important. Some breeds, typically those originating from cold northern climates such as sled dogs, have a coarse outer coat and a dense inner layer of fur, which traps warm air close to the body. At the other extreme, breeds whose

ancestry lies close to the equator have thin coats with virtually no undercoat—so Chihuahuas are vulnerable to the cold both because of their size and their coat type.

If your pet starts to shiver indoors, it is not necessarily a sign that he is cold. If he starts to follow you around while shivering, it is much more likely to be a sign that he is excited, perhaps in anticipation of a meal or a walk. Shivering can also be an indication of fear or shock, particularly after an encounter with a larger, aggressive animal.

Smiling

Dogs sometimes show a distinctive facial gesture, which looks very much like a smile. The lips are drawn back, but without exposing any teeth, since this would then be a sign of aggression. This "smile" is actually a gesture of appeasement, so you are most likely to see your pet behave in this way after you have told him off. The smile is often followed by a yawn, which is your dog's way of relieving the tension of the situation.

Soiling

The cause for this could be medical—perhaps an infection of the urinary tract—or alternatively it could be behavioral. On the other hand, it may be much simpler—you may just have forgotten to let your dog out when he needed to go, so he had no choice but to soil in the home. Young dogs are unlikely to ask to go out, because they will not be fully toilet-trained until six months of age.

Male dogs who soil repeatedly around the home are likely to be doing so as a territorial marker, so you will probably see a very rapid improvement if your pet is neutered. After an instance of soiling, thorough cleaning of the area is recommended (see page 180) to prevent your pet from returning to the same area over and over to relieve himself.

See also Urination (Uncontrolled).

Stealing Food

This is a common problem with most dogs because they are natural scavengers. It is not just a matter of making sure your pet cannot leap up on to the table to steal food, you also need to put shopping away rather than leaving it in bags on the floor within your pet's reach. Items such as chocolate could make your pet very ill and might even be fatal.

Symptoms of Sickness

Dogs may be sick for a variety of reasons, but it may not be a sign of illness. Bitches often vomit up food for their puppies as they approach the weaning stage—such behavior is quite normal, although it appears unpleasant to us. Puppies find it easier to absorb their mother's predigested food; similar behavior is commonplace in their gray wolf ancestor. Dogs also vomit to cleanse out their system if they have eaten something unpleasant, which can help to prevent an animal becoming more seriously ill if he has consumed food heavily contaminated by bacteria. In such cases it is usually sufficient to ensure that your pet receives only a light meal for a day or so, until he

has recovered. However, if he is afflicted by diarrhea as well, he may be vulnerable to dehydration, so you should seek advice from your veterinarian—particularly in the case of young or old dogs. Some dogs eat stems of grass to make themselves sick, which can often be linked with the presence of worms in the gut. If your dog persists in behaving in this way and you have not dewormed him recently, deworming tablets can resolve the problem.

If your dog is retching but not actually vomiting, it is possible that he has swallowed a piece of bone or a similar item that is causing a partial obstruction in his throat. Investigate without delay, although you may not be able to spot the offending item, and if the problem persists take him to your vet.
See also Grass (Eating), Fever, Illness, Parasites.

T

Tail Chasing

Puppies often chase their own tails, especially after they are separated from their littermates; it is a way of playing on their own. In most cases a young dog will soon grow out of this phase, but in a few cases it can develop into part of the dog's regular pattern of behavior.

In some circumstances tail-chasing is a sign of boredom, but if you provide your dog with a suitable range of toys, he will start to amuse himself with them instead. When tail-chasing, your dog will pursue the tip of the tail, but if your pet is twisting around to try to nibble at the base of the tail, this indicates a problem. He is trying to relieve pain or irritation here, caused by impacted anal glands or even fleas.
See also Nibbling at Skin, Scratching (Himself).

Tiredness

Take special care when exercising older dogs, especially if they are suffering from hip dysplasia or other joint ailments that can make walking difficult. If you notice that your pet is lagging behind and having difficulty keeping up with you, stop and head slowly back. He is indicating that he is tired and may be suffering from joint pain as well, particularly if he is limping. With this type of ailment, some days can be better than others for your pet. The weather also plays a part in this: Cold, wet conditions are likely to make walking more painful for dogs that experience joint pain than when the weather is warm and sunny.

See also Exercise, Lethargy.

Toys

Dogs should be trained from an early age to give up toys on the command "Drop." At first a puppy may not realize what is required, but if you open your pet's mouth gently to take the toy away, he will soon learn. Dogs enjoy having a range of toys to play with, both to chew and to chase after, and usually are happy to play a game.

Take care with an unneutered bitch about two months after her season; at this stage her behavior may change dramatically, and she may suddenly become highly protective toward a favored toy, growling ferociously and even snapping if you try to take it away. This is a sign of a phantom pregnancy, a condition in which hormonal changes in the bitch's body mimic the signs of pregnancy—even to the extent of milk production in some cases, although she has not mated at the appropriate time. As a result of all these factors, however, she now regards the toy as a puppy, which she is intent on protecting and will defend fiercely if she thinks you are trying to remove it from her.

Although this phase will eventually pass, veterinary treatment may be necessary to alleviate the worst of the symptoms—ultimately, the long-term solution is to have your pet neutered.

U

Urination (Uncontrolled)

Young dogs need to be trained not to soil around the home, and this is usually straightforward, using a combination of puppy training pads and cleaning up thoroughly when a puppy goes in the wrong place, indoors or out. However, things may not always proceed smoothly despite even your best efforts, causing you to have serious concerns about why your puppy is so willful.

In certain breeds, such as the West Highland white terrier and Labrador retriever, puppies are born with a defect that means one or both ureters—which connect the kidney with the bladder—are misplaced. The result is that urine bypasses the bladder and flows directly out of the body. The problem will be apparent in puppies from three months of age onward, with bitches far more commonly affected than male dogs. Your vet will be able to test for this condition, which is known as an ectopic ureter, and it can be corrected by surgery.
See also Soiling.

V

Visitors

There are times when it can be very helpful if your dog barks—such as when a stranger is approaching your property. However, you do not want your dog to continue barking repeatedly whenever a visitor calls, causing a disturbance to the entire neighborhood. Generally, a dog will soon quiet down after an initial period of barking—particularly if he can see that you are not concerned by the other person's presence—but training is also very important. To deter a puppy from barking persistently, allow your visitor to say hello and then distract your dog's attention by encouraging him to sit down. Then, after the initial phase of excitement has passed, the puppy will quite often fall asleep.

It is important to socialize puppies with people, both in and outside your home, to make sure that your dog will not grow up to be nervous around company. Certain types of dog, such as sight hounds, are often instinctively shyer than those that were evolved to work closely alongside people, such as the various retrievers, who accept the company of strangers more readily.

W

Whining

This is a call demanding attention, often made when you are about to feed your pet and becoming louder and more frequent if you ignore it. The solution, as far as food is concerned, is not to delay feeding your dog.

Investigate if your dog starts to whine unexpectedly—he may be trapped in a room, unable to open the door, or it may simply be that a favorite toy or ball has rolled out of reach. Dogs sometimes whine in the car on the way to a walk as a sign of impatience. If your pet persists in behaving this way, take him out for short drives that do not end in a walk to convince him that he is not always going to have a walk after traveling in the car.
See also Attention Seeking.

Accidents

With the increasing number of vehicles on the roads today, keeping your dog under control at all times and trying to anticipate danger is very important. Dogs generally display no road sense—although as part of their training on the leash, you should encourage them to sit before walking across the road when it is clear. This can help to instill a sense of danger. Find safe areas where you can allow your dog to run freely when you are exercising him off the leash. Take special care with young dogs, who may run off without warning if they spot something interesting in the distance. At home you must also be alert—develop a routine of shutting your dog in an area where he cannot run out onto the road if the front door is left open.

If an accident happens

Unfortunately, dogs are injured or even killed quite regularly due to collisions with vehicles. It will be a distressing experience if you ever witness an accident, even if your dog is not involved. However, if you can overcome your sense of horror and act promptly, it will increase the possibility of veterinary assistance saving the dog's life, depending on the severity of his injuries.

A dog will be badly shocked and distressed after an accident, which may cause him to act aggressively even if he knows you well. If he is still able to walk after the collision, the first thing to do is to catch him. He may have lost his collar or may not be wearing one if he is a stray dog, but if you have a leash, you may be able to use this as a lasso around his neck. A length of rope can also be used, some other form of tie, or even hosiery in the short term. After restraining the dog, you need to move him away from danger as quickly as possible. Take care to avoid being hit yourself if you have to dart around moving vehicles—the drivers may not even be aware that a collision has taken place.

A different approach is required if the dog is lying in the road after being hit. Although your initial reaction may be to try to help him where he has fallen, the most important thing is to move him carefully away from the traffic. Never tip the body of an injured dog when you are moving him, because if the diaphragm that partitions the chest and abdomen has been torn, the body organs can be seriously displaced and the injury could be worsened. If he is unconscious, you may be able to pick him up by placing your hands under his body and carrying him in a horizontal position to the roadside. Shock and loss of consciousness may result in the dog losing his bladder and bowel tone, so be aware of this possibility when you are moving him—ideally, hold his rear end away from you. A large dog can be slid onto a blanket or something similar, then moved with four people each taking a corner.

On the sidewalk

Once the dog is safely away from danger, check to see if he is still breathing even if he has lost consciousness. Check for a pulse, although this may be hard to find. Flex the elbow up onto the left-hand side of the body, which will give you the approximate position of the heart—you should be able to feel a pulse here. The other area to try is the femoral artery at the top on the inside of the hind leg, which may be easier if a dog has long hair. Move your finger slowly over the area, but do not press down hard, because this will mask the vibration. It is a good idea to practice taking your dog's pulse so that in an emergency you can locate it easily. If the dog's heart has stopped, press up and down on the rib cage above the heart (with the dog lying on his right-hand side), counting to five, to try to start it again. This may not be possible, though, if there is an obvious injury to the chest.

Blocked airway

Check that the dog has not swallowed his tongue if he is unconscious, because this could obstruct the airway and prevent him from breathing. Open his mouth carefully so you can pull the tongue forward without being bitten. If you are in an area where rabies is endemic and it is not your dog, it is safer to use a stick for this so you do not come into direct contact with saliva that may contain the virus. The danger from rabies is also why it is not recommended to give mouth-to-mouth artificial respiration.

Stemming blood loss

After an accident, the dog may suffer severe bleeding. The most effective way to stem blood flow is to wrap the area as much as possible in a bandage of some kind. Choose clean material for this and seek veterinary help immediately.

Longer-term consequences

If the dog is a stray, there may be an animal rescue service that you can call for help. If your pet has been hit, seek advice from your veterinarian immediately. You will probably need to take your dog to their surgery unit so he can be checked over carefully; the severity of injuries resulting from an accident may not be immediately apparent in the aftermath, particularly if there is internal hemorrhaging. Even if your dog appears unaffected, a checkup is still advisable because his condition may deteriorate unexpectedly, placing his life in danger.

If there is a fracture, there are ways of stabilizing the broken bone so it will heal cleanly—x-ray images will allow your veterinarian to assess the severity of the injury. There are often trauma injuries to the skin as well, but although these frequently look serious, there is a good chance that they can be repaired successfully, providing the wound does not become infected. In some cases it may be necessary to graft skin across the damaged area.

Poisoning

A wide variety of substances can be harmful to dogs, including items that may seem innocuous to us, such as chocolate. A dog who eats chocolate is at serious risk from theobromine poisoning, which is likely to result in respiratory failure. The impact of poisons can be very diverse, so poisoning should always be suspected if your dog suddenly appears ill or starts to act strangely. Antifreeze is especially dangerous, so never allow your dog to be unsupervised in a garage where he might drink this chemical in mistake for water. As a guide, as little as 1 oz. (30 ml) of antifreeze can be fatal for a dog weighing 15 lb. (7 kg).

If you know your dog has ingested a potentially poisonous substance, seek your vet's advice immediately, providing as much information as possible about what and how much has been consumed. Note that it is not necessarily a good idea to encourage your dog to vomit under these circumstances.

Heat stroke

A dog who has collapsed from heat stroke is in a serious condition. You need to lower his body temperature rapidly—dousing him with cold water or, better still, hosing him down in a bath should prevent a fatal outcome. There should be an improvement within five minutes or so, and the dog will probably need a drink soon afterward.

Your Dog's Hidden Past

The following charts indicate the original purpose for which breeds were created, which often still influences their personalities today.

Toy-Sized Dogs

Not surprisingly, many small dogs were originally bred as pets, but do not rely on size alone as a fail-safe method of determining their level of activity. Many terriers have very active natures and are best suited to a rural environment, where their instincts to explore will be very evident. Kept confined in the home, they can easily become bored and are then likely to be destructive. Most of the true companion breeds have an ancestry that dates back centuries, however, which ensures they generally settle well in domestic surroundings and instinctively form a close bond with those in their immediate family.

Breed	Purpose
Affenpinscher	hunting rodents
Australian silky terrier	companion
Bichon frise	royal companion
Border terrier	flushing foxes
Cairn terrier	flushing foxes
Chihuahua	companion
Chinese crested dog	companion
Continental toy spaniel	companion
Dachshund	hunting badgers
Dandie dinmont terrier	hunting rats
French bulldog	companion
Griffon bruxellois	hunting rats
Havanese	companion
Japanese chin	aristocratic companion

Breed	Purpose
King Charles spaniel	royal companion
Norfolk terrier	hunting rats
Pekingese	aristocratic companion
Pomeranian	companion
Pug	companion
Scottish terrier	hunting rats
Sealyham terrier	hunting badgers and otters
Shih tzu	aristocratic companion
Skye terrier	hunting badgers and foxes
Tibetan spaniel	monastic companion
Welsh corgi	cattle drover
West Highland white terrier	hunting rats
Yorkshire terrier	hunting rats

Small Dogs

This group consists of smaller hounds and gundogs, as well as the larger terriers. Due to their small size, many of these breeds were developed as hunting companions, but some are scaled-down versions of larger dogs, such as the Italian greyhound, which has always been a companion and needs far less exercise in general than most of the other dogs listed here. Their size means that members of this group can be picked up and carried quite easily, which can be an important consideration in some situations but may be easily overlooked at the outset, particularly with a puppy.

Breed	Original purpose
American cocker spaniel	gundog, retrieving quail
Basenji	all-purpose hunting dog
Basset Griffon Vendeen	hunting hares and rabbits
Basset hound	hunting hares and rabbits
Beagle	hunting hares and rabbits
Bedlington terrier	hunting rats and badgers
Boston terrier	fighting breed
Bulldog	bull-baiting
Cavalier King Charles spaniel	companion
Chow chow	guardian, cart-puller
Cocker spaniel	gundog, flushing woodcock
Coton de Tulear	companion
Finnish spitz	hunting birds
Fox terrier	flushing foxes
Glen of Imaal terrier	hunting rats
Hungarian puli	sheep herding
Inca hairless dog	bed-warmer
Italian greyhound	companion
Keeshond	barge watchdog
Lancashire Heeler	hunting rats
Lhasa apso	monastic companion
Lowchen	aristocratic companion
Norwegian buhund	stock herding
Parson Jack Russell terrier	flushing foxes
Polish lowland sheepdog	sheep herding
Poodle (standard)	retrieving from water
Schipperke	barge watchdog
Shar-pei	dogfighting
Shetland sheepdog	sheep herding
Staffordshire bull terrier	dogfighting
Swedish vallhund	cattle drover
Tibetan terrier	stock herding, guardian
Welsh terrier	hunting rats
Whippet	dog racing

Medium-Sized Dogs

Many of these dogs were bred to herd farmstock or act as retrievers, which means that they instinctively form a close bond with people. This in turn is likely to make training them much easier. Most members of this category are lively and energetic, so be prepared for relatively lengthy walks every day. The majority are not well suited to urban living, where they may be expected simply to trot around a park.

Breed	Purpose
Airedale terrier	hunting badgers and otters
Australian cattle dog	herding cattle
Australian shepherd	sheep herding
Bearded collie	sheep herding
Bluetick coonhound	hunting raccoons
Border collie	sheep herding
Boxer	bull-baiting, guard dog
Brittany	retriever
Bull terrier	bull-baiting, ratting
Canaan dog	feral, livestock guardian
Catahoula leopard dog	pig and cattle drover
Collies (rough and smooth)	sheep herding
Dalmatian	carriage dog
Elkhound	hunting elk
English springer spaniel	flushing game
Flat-coated retriever	retrieving waterfowl
German shepherd dog	sheep herding
Golden retriever	retrieving birds
Haldenstovare	tracking game
Hamiltonstovare	tracking game
Harrier	hunting hares
Ibizan hound	hunting rabbits
Irish setter	retrieving game
Irish water spaniel	retrieving waterfowl
Italian hound	hunting
Kai dog	hunting wild boar and deer
Kerry beagle	hunting hares
Kerry blue terrier	hunting rats
Kuvasz	flock guardian
Labrador retriever	fisherman's dog
Large munsterlander	locating and retrieving game
Nova Scotia duck tolling retriever	waterfowl lure and retriever
Old English sheepdog	sheep herding
Portuguese water dog	fisherman's dog
Sabueso Espanol	tracking game
Siberian husky	sled dog
Sicilian greyhound	hunting rabbits
Soft-coated wheaten terrier	cattle drover, ratter
Welsh springer spaniel	flushing ("springing") game

Large Dogs

These are strong dogs, with powerful personalities in many cases. A number have been developed as guardians, while others were originally created as flock guardians and some were evolved for hunting purposes. This diversity in origins again emphasizes the need to look carefully into a breed's background, because this influences not just its personality but also the way in which it should be kept and trained. Some breeds, such as the rottweiler, are likely to be much more intimidating than others, such as the mild-mannered greyhound. The size of the members of this group, combined with their generally exuberant natures, means that they are not necessarily a good choice for a home with toddlers.

Afghan hound	hunting wolves and gazelles	Bull mastiff	estate guardian
Akita	dog fighting	Chesapeake Bay retriever	retrieving waterfowl
Alaskan Malamute	sled dog	Curly-coated retriever	retrieving waterfowl
American foxhound	hunting foxes	Doberman	guardian
Anatolian shepherd dog	sheep guardian	Dogo Argentino	hunting jaguars and pumas
Auvergne pointer	pointing and retrieving game	Dogue de Bordeaux	guardian, hunting game
Azawakh	hunting gazelles	English setter	locating and retrieving birds
Beauceron	hunting wild boar	Fila Brasileiro	tracking down escaped slaves
Belgian shepherd dogs : Groenendael/Laekenois / Malinois/Teruveren	stock herding	Foxhound	hunting foxes
Berger de Picard	sheep herding	German pointer	pointing and retrieving
Bernese mountain dog	pulling carts	Giant schnauzer	cattle drover
Black and tan coonhound	hunting raccoons	Gordon setter	retrieving birds
Black Russian terrier	military guard dog	Great Pyrenees	flock guardian
Bloodhound	tracking	Great Swiss mountain dog	pulling carts
Borzoi	hunting wolves	Greyhound	hunting game
Bouvier des Flandres	cattle drover	Ibizan hound	hunting rabbits
Briard	flock guardian, herding	Italian spinone	retrieving game

Kuvasz	flock guardian		Rottweiler	cattle drover, guardian
Lurcher	hunting hares		Saarlooswolfhond	breeding experiment
Magyar agar	hunting game		St. Bernard	search and rescue work
Maremma sheepdog	flock guardian		Saluki	hunting gazelles
Mastiff	guard dog		Sloughi	flock guardian, hunter
Neapolitan mastiff	guard dog, dog fighting		Spanish greyhound	hunting game, racing
Newfoundland	fisherman's dog		Spanish mastiff	flock guardian
Otterhound	hunting otters		Spanish pointer	pointing and retrieving
Pharaoh hound	hunting rabbits		Tibetan mastiff	flock guardian
Pointer	pointing and retrieving game		Tosa inu	dogfighting
Polish hound	hunting large game		Vizsla	hunting and retrieving game
Rafeiro do Alentejo	guard dog		Weimaraner	tracking game
Rhodesian ridgeback	hunting lions			

Giant Dogs

Members of this group may be the largest dogs in the world today, but as a study of their ancestries reveal, these are not aggressive dogs by nature, in spite of their size. Even so, they need plenty of space for exercise, and they can be intimidating, although in reality, an Irish wolfhound, for example, is more likely to lick you to death than to savage you! For reasons that are not clear, however, these giant dogs have a shorter lifespan on average than the toy breeds at the opposite end of the size scale, and they have a relatively high risk of suffering bone cancer, affecting the legs.

Deerhound	hunting deer		Landseer	fisherman's companion
Great Dane	hunting large game		Leonberger	symbolic mascot
Irish wolfhound	hunting wolves		Pyrenean mastiff	flock guardian
Komondor	flock guardian			

index

Photo credits